THE LITTLE WORLD

by

STELLA BENSON

Contents

TRIPPERS

In Tintagel Cove the sea is as luminously green as though it had a light beneath it. The rocks above water are like leopards, streaked and spotted, and beneath the water they are like pale tremulous green ghosts. There is another ghost sometimes in the water; sometimes it comes to the surface and becomes a seal. The seal looks nervously this way and that; it looks first outward at the safe sea and then inward at the beach all flowered with the jumpers of charabankers. When it sees the jumpers it dives hurriedly and only reappears now and then to confirm its worst fears.

The broken indented outlines of King Arthur's Castle comb the mists which stream in from the sea. The Castle crowns a high solitary rock and there is only one way on to the rock. It is a steep way only to be followed by nimble trippers in single file.

This is a piece of pretence history and concerns the nimblest trippers of all. Being history it points no moral except the obvious moral that it is no wiser to be born within earshot of Piccadilly than without.

The nimble Piccadilly trippers were four in number and they got up at four o'clock in the morning of Bank Holiday. One carried a large bowl of Cornish cream; one carried a sack of saffron cakes, one a crate of pasties and the fourth was armed to the teeth. They were desperate persons and their names were Mirabeau and Mirabel, Justin and Justine. They belonged to the most subtle and insidious type of tripper. Justine and Mirabel wore neither orange jumpers nor bandanas. They were plain-clothes trippers and they were not only desperate but exceedingly supercilious.

There is a very small old lady who keeps the keys of the Castle. She knows a great deal about trippers—she laughs at them, but I do not think she finds it necessary to despise them. She is a Resident, and residents shall inherit the earth. She did not know enough to suspect the four super-trippers, Mirabeau and Mirabel, Justin and Justine. Armed with the key they filed along the steep sloping ridge that leads to the Castle gate. Perhaps the ghost of the fair bridge across which Lancelot rode still hung upon the air above their heads but, as a support for the feet of trippers, that bridge has gone. One must climb down now, down almost within reach of the springing apple-green spray, almost within earshot of the drumming of the sea in the caves below the Castle—and then up again towards a sky patterned with white castle-clouds and with a changing design of seagulls.

When the time of day changed from faery time to human time— that is to say, at about nine o'clock—there was a roaring sound that at first was like a little seed of sound planted in the air, but presently outgrew even the chanting of the sea. And along every road—from Newquay, from Clovelly, from Bude and Bodmin, from Plymouth and the two St. Columbs—from farther afield still, I think—from Kilburn, Walthamstow and the two Tootings, from Birmingham and the raucous streets of Liverpool and Glasgow, from New York and Philadelphia and the bald yellow cities of Illinois—came the charabancs, carrying hosts of the most innocent and terrible enemy of all, massing for the last spoiling of the Castle.

"Trippers," said Mirabeau, as he balanced the last of a row of quartz-and crystal-shot boulders on the brink of the precipice, "devour the colour of the sea and bring the sun of the suburbs into the green dark of caves. Even fine weather is dull because they prayed for it in church yesterday."

"Trippers," said Justin who, with muscular yet refined movements, was driving stakes across the door in the machicolated wall, "are the last proof of the first fall from grace. Nobody tripped before Adam and Eve fell—or, in other words, before the first conducted tour was made from the first garden suburb."

Mirabel was stacking provisions in a little cave under a bank of thyme. She said, "I hate trippers senselessly. I hate their women because their blouses are thicker and more vivid than their skirts, because their skirts dip behind and because they lie in gross lumps upon the thyme with their hats awry. I hate the men because their coats are not Harris tweed yet pretend to be, and because their shoes are the wrong brown. I hate little children with chocolate round their mouths and no handkerchiefs. I hate them all because they play gramophones in places where not even music should intrude. I know well that every one has a right to the air that blows over the peacock sea—even if

2

some people breathe that air through sticks of peppermint rock. I admit I am a tripper myself; I come from far to see things I have heard of. To eat lotus in a Chinese temple garden or bananas on Blackpool pier is the same thing—I know it. But I am I and only I have rights."

Justine said nothing, but she covered with her revolver the leaders of the long line of trippers filing up the path that grooves the first boulders at the foot of the Castle rock. The leading tripper was a woman in a striped blouse and flounced skirt; she was inadequately corseted yet very warm. Two little girls followed her; they wore thick red dresses with low waists and lace collars; their cheeks bulged with bull's-eyes. Behind them came a man with a fat cheerful nose and a curl on his forehead; he wore his cap back to front.

As Mirabeau and Justin set their shoulders to the first balanced boulder, Justine pulled the trigger and Mirabel unfurled their banner in the misty wind.

The police from Launceston, sent for by a distracted Parish council, found the four supercilious super-trippers after the siege was broken. They lay in the King's Chapel on the summit of their stronghold—the four silly crusaders. They lay in a row with their sneering eyes shut and their knees crossed—like other crusaders.

Their souls were shaking hands with King Arthur and his knights in Paradise.
"Come in, adventurers," cried Arthur, "trippers all, come in." And when he had shaken hands with Mirabeau and Mirabel, Justin and Justine, he turned with outstretched hand to the other trippers asthmatically filing up the quartz-shot path to Paradise. There was the hot woman, striped and sticky as a bull's-eye; there was the imitation motor-cyclist with his cap the wrong way round, and there were the little girls with remnants of chocolate clinging to their very eyelashes.
"Come in, come in, adventurers all...."

3

OLDEST INHABITANTS

I think of starting a simple but expensive memory course for inhabitants of the provinces of over eighty years of age. Oldest inhabitants seem to be always culled from our rural population. One very rarely meets a Londoner who remembers Piccadilly Circus before Mercury—(or is it Eros?)—alighted there, or Kensington before Barker's arrival, or the Underground before it knew Pears' Soap. Londoners have either short memories or short lives. My memory course, therefore, will advertise for its public in the provinces only. The advertisements will be headed "Too YOUNG AT SEVENTY?" Pupils will be expected to commit to memory simple incidents connected with the Napoleonic Wars—(including the reports current weekly of Napoleon's execution in the Tower)—the first journey of Puffing Billy—(tickets obtainable from Thomas Cook's grandfather and Son's great-grandfather)—and the laying of a wreath on the grave of George IV. by the secretary of the Upward and Onward Society.

A cheaper line for juniors will embrace the Crimean War, the first penny stamp and humorous anecdotes about aunts in crinolines and uncles on boneshaker bicycles. Those who wish to specialise in having spoken with the son of the man who was the first to spread the news of Queen Anne's death, or having been dandled on the knee of the great-granddaughter of the barmaid who served the last drink to Ben Jonson, may do so at a higher rate.

Everyone is a potential Oldest Inhabitant—more or less consciously. Throughout the War and the Peace and the drought and the strikes—even in the dim days of Suffragette trouble or the first motor-cars—you could see budding Oldest Inhabitants going about with pursed lips thinking, "By Jove, won't it be fun to tell my great-grandchildren this.... My, won't they gape...." As a matter of fact, great-grandchildren never gape; they walk away when reminiscences begin. Indeed at the present time nobody walks away more quickly than I do. But I cannot conceal from myself the fact that the day must come when I no longer walk away but, on the contrary, am walked away from.

However it is fortunate that Oldest Inhabitants do not have to depend on their great-grandchildren for the necessary half-crowns. As long as a journalist is left alive Oldest Inhabitants will never find themselves without a public.

I myself mean to out-reminisce the most ardent reminiscer. Already, while yet most of my carefully stored copy is shared with every man in the street, when nobody wants to hear my air-raid adventures, when nobody will admire me for drinking sugarless coffee in 1916, when, in a word, everyone knows far too much—I am beset by temptation. Everyone is; that is why so many of us go to America now and it is also why so many Americans are coming over here. They can still nail our attention by means of anecdotes of Prohibition, and we can still raise a thrill in the States by lying about bombs. But these triumphs are too easy for me. I find that as the years pass my tendency is to have been actually and actively present at every great event in the world's history during the last twenty-five years. Yesterday my friends might have heard me mention that I had seen the first aeroplane that flew at Aldershot, lived in the same world as Tennyson, Gladstone and Dan Leno, watched on the Barbary Coast the first scenes of the tragedy of Prohibition. To-morrow—or, more accurately, in the year 2000—there is no saying what my friends may hear me mention. By then I shall have looped the loop with Cody and Count Zeppelin, I shall have heard Tennyson recite the "Idylls of the King" to the Fabian Society, I shall have shared with Gladstone at Delmonico's, N.Y., the last recorded cocktail in the States. "That was the year of the drought," I shall add triumphantly, "the year when all the best people could be seen going down Piccadilly in aertex-cellular lounge suits made by Mr. Mallaby-Deeley...." I shall really believe it. The mind's eye is a docile organ.

If all this should not come true of me, then no doubt it will be true of you. Nearly all of us are really counting on becoming Oldest Inhabitants. We all have our little pet lies laid by in lavender.

THE STATES—I

My friend and I had come—walking and borrowing "lifts" alternately—up to this mountain village in New England because there was a house there that had once been hers and because she wanted to revisit a place she remembered and loved. But the place didn't smile in the same way as she remembered—places never do; her own late house was empty of hospitable successors and the village had forgotten her. We broke into the empty house and stayed in it for a night or two, finding some marooned cans of pork and beans in the larder. On Sunday we went, on an impulse, to church, seeking distraction. The impulse had seized my friend immediately after she had washed her hair, and church saw us arriving, she with towelled shoulders and a handsome disorder of dripping yellow hair down her back, I in smock, breeches and a little sat-upon hat. I remembered church in my English youth—Sunday hats, and tight shoes squeaking up the aisle—and hoped that the Almighty would prove to be more democratic in this His Own Country. He did. The minister vaulted from his dais to welcome us and, taking one of our hands in each of his, drew us to a front pew.

"Now which of you plays the harmawnium?" he said to us archly. "Our organist has failed us."

"*She* does. She's English," said my friend, in consequence almost ceasing to be my friend for the moment.

"Now isn't that just *fine*," said the minister, and drew me out of the pew towards the harmonium.

Now I have never tried to play the harmonium, but on the piano, the guitar or the penny whistle I can play "Abide with Me" or "Sun of my Soul" rather well. Unfortunately, as this was a morning service, the shades of night could not be expected to bear out the spirit of these hymns, but the minister, on being informed of my musical limitations, said that this was not really very important.

So after a moment of silent stage fright, during which I could hear no sound but the regular dripping of my friend's hair on the back of her pew, I began, intending to play a few preliminary staves of the hymn, solo, as they do in all the best abbeys and cathedrals. The congregation appreciated this intention but the minister did not. He began Abiding with Me from the first note, leaving the congregation to burst into tongue two lines later. There was a terrible entanglement of sound which indeed was never unravelled before the end of the hymn, for I could not make up my mind which to follow. I returned to my pew without waiting for an encore.

But the minister forgave me. He inserted into his sermon a generous and hearty testimonial to England and the English.

"A nawble race, the English," he said and leaned over towards me for confirmation. "Isn't that saw?... Empire, I believe, does not necessarily spring from imperialism ... dawn't you agree with me?... and now that we are all engaged in the greatest international conflict in history, dawn't you think we ought ..."

These appeals were addressed directly to me and, since I had never taken part in a sermon before in this way, I hardly knew whether I was right in replying, "Indeed I hope so ... yes certainly ... no doubt you are right," etc., etc. I now think that the questions were simply rhetorical, though they did not seem so, and that a gratified silence was all that was expected of me.

After this scene of humiliation we decided to seek oblivion in departure. Hearing that a train was to leave its terminus eighteen miles away at sunrise next morning, we determined to walk all night and catch it.

We took two blankets from the linen cupboard of the house in which we had been making an unauthorised visit, a lantern, and a horrible cocktail made of the dregs of a whisky bottle mixed with those of a brandy bottle. (The cellar of our unknown hosts was lamentably low.) We thought that this mixture might at least save our lives in an emergency. We wore the blankets as ponchos.

"At least," said my friend, as we set off in the bright moonlight looking like two ambulant bolsters, "we're *safe* anywhere. Dressed like this we needn't fear that we shall fascinate the licentious peasantry."

7

Nothing happened to us. We walked all night down empty frosty moonlit roads. We strayed four miles out of our way and found ourselves among the great fantastic buildings of a deserted iron foundry. Huge pale towers and halls seemed to have been built by an extinct race of giants. One imagined that they were only reconstructed on the remembering air when the old moon shone full. For a time we could find no-one, not even a ghost, to set us on our way again, but presently we found a solitary post office, and our clamour woke up a tolerant postmaster who came out, dressed in a childish night-dress, and showed us our path.

The moonlight at last was strangely replaced by a clear frosty dawn, and as soon as commonplace daylight stripped the far valleys of mist and mysteries, we saw our train standing, puffing urgently, a thousand miles away, as it seemed. So we ran. We ran downhill for the whole thousand miles. I thought I should never breathe again. The poncho and the frightful cocktail somehow induced me to break out into a violent cold sweat—a thing I had read about but never experienced. I froze and dripped simultaneously. I was sure that death must follow this effort, but still it seemed worth it if we could catch that train. A car passed us and answered our wavings and entreaties for a lift with "Git out the road." We reached the depot as the tail of the train disappeared round the bend. Twenty-one miles of violent endeavour wasted. Defeated and robbed of pride we threw ourselves on our backs in mid-platform. The depot men stood round us, eyeing our disguise, scarcely believing their eyes. The driver of the car that had passed us came and said, "Werl ... wurn't that too bad. I ses to meself, 'Ef I knoo who them two females was I'd take a chance and givem a lift to the depot' ... But you sure looked so queer and I ses to meself, 'One can never tell' ..."

The innkeeper of that village was a jewel. He gave us quantities of brandy—at five o'clock in the morning—he boiled hot baths with his own hands. There was no train that day and we slept under six quilts each till the night. But when we sought to pay our bill the landlord said, "Aw werl ... I dawn't take money from fawks that looks as ef they hadn't got enough of it."

We nearly missed the next train in our efforts to induce him to compromise.

THE STATES—II

I never could make any impression on American newspapers. They never hailed me as a contributor; even as an interviewee I cut no ice. What I hoped were the subtler intricacies of my character seemed always to be missed by interviewers. "She Hit a London Cop" was once printed under my photograph to give point to an interview in which I had given rein to my opinions on the Feminist question. The truth is, we English are not dramatic enough; the English affectation or art of understatement makes absolutely no appeal in America. The essence of American art and wit is overstatement.

Studying the most serious news-organ of San Francisco, streaked with comics, spotted with movie darlings and murderers, patched with eye-stretching domestic secrets like—HUBBY NEVER COMES HOME TILL BREAKFAST SAYS FAIR PLEADER,—I used to remember the sacred sheet upon my London breakfast-table of long ago, reticent, unsmiling, scrupulously unlocal, innocent of large type, hiding its light under a bushel of refined advertisement, leaving nothing outside for the superficial eye but the triple mystery—birth, death and marriage....

American papers are meant to be read in one minute by people who have only two minutes of leisure during the day and spend them in an elevator on the way to the office. They have to atone for their garrulity by an extreme concentration of snappy news on their outer pages. For instance, the democratic American, wishing to know which of his social superiors is in town, can master at a glance this information in type three inches high at the head of an outside column—GEE THIS IS GREAT SAYS WOOL KING HOME FROM WILDS. Whereas the democratic Englishman on a similar quest would probably go all the way from Mornington Crescent to Elephant and Castle before he found the following treasure buried in the insignificant masses of the Court Circular: *Mr. and Mrs. Marmaduke Woolley have returned to their town residence after a visit to the country.* Or again, the belligerent American hungering to stretch his lungs once more to the tune of "The Star-Spangled Banner"—in which exercise he was so prematurely interrupted in 1918—may be gratified by this six-inch statement:—WAR WITH SO-AND-SO INEVITABLE,—without troubling to lower his busy and patriotic eye to the tiresome postscript in the smallest possible lettering—*is opinion of Mayor of Minxville.*

The American newspaper often consists of as much as half a column devoted to international affairs, an immense auto section, a financial section, a movie section, a society section showing Native Sons and Daughters of the Golden West in sepia attending each other's weddings, and a scandal section describing the deliciously immoral practices of minor European princelings whom no-one ever heard of before. These scandal supplements inspire and excuse such opinions as that with which one of my pupils in a California university once began his essay: *All foreigners labour under crowned heads in dirt and immortality.* There is also, in a well-conducted newspaper, a woman's section, a supplement devoted to the private affairs of the Prince of Wales, a baseball section, a supplement for the instruction of our kiddies, and a Love Supplement (the illustrated story of the Love of Goldlashes and her Soldier Boy throughout the ages). Above all there is the Comic Supplement.

One of the most uniting elements in the United States is the Comic Supplement. Every city has its newspapers; no city reads the organ of any other city, but the comics are common to all respectable newspapers and one may help to Bring Up Father anywhere between the Atlantic and the Pacific. *Father* is the angel of America, *Maggie* stands for devil. *Father* has a very much greater and more loyal band of followers than has the President of the United States. What *Father* says—*goes.*

I have only once known the comics to miss their mark, and that—I am ashamed to say—was in a certain neighbourhood peopled by a little English colony of ranchers and miners at the foot of the Rockies in Colorado. I lived there for some months doing odd chores for a kind old English couple. I loaded alfalfa or delivered butter and eggs in the little mining city five miles off all day, and at night—since the shack was only a two-room one—slept comfortably and healthily on the porch with snow drifting over me. But at meals and in the evenings we had heart to heart talks in the little hot cramped kitchen-livingroom; we discussed the Comic Supplements—from a moral standpoint.

"She didn't ought to 'ave clipped 'im one on the jaw.... A woman's a woman, meant to love, honour and obey, and there ain't no excuse for a woman be'aving like that.... Oh yes—I know 'e provoked 'er, men can be a sore trial and that's a fact—but still...."

In the presence of any great natural phenomenon such as Niagara or Bringing Up Father, it becomes at once apparent how incurably man suffers from inadequacy—and perhaps the English more than any other race, on account of their craving for cold moderation in words. I once made an expedition up a Rocky Mountain with these same ranching compatriots and some neighbours who were miners. There was a view, east, of the prairie, west, of the white peaks; there were, at our feet, fantastic sloping rocks of a rare true rose-red. When we saw these things we all looked ashamed as if God had been mentioned. Then we said, "My word, I can see Harrison's shack quite plain. And there now ... if I can't see the pigstye be'ind it. See that little speck? That must be the 'og that 'e looks to kill come Saturday...." But we soon turned from that to a discussion of a Royal Prince's marriage.

And I must say that not one of the Americans about us on that mountain top seemed to be writing odes or praising God.

Americans travel as tourists, we travel as money-seekers. But— and here is the strange thing—we all come home at last as poets. Man is only articulate when his thoughts run home. The American on the beautiful other side of the world forgets liberty and George Washington and remembers the good ground on which he once set his feet, the deep shadows across his canyons, the cactus on his warm foothills, the steep ladders of sunlight on Fifth Avenue. And the Englishman, bound by the chains of property in the shadow of alien mountains, forgets the dust kicked up by the charabancs, forgets the high income tax, seeks reminders only of the little poetic things of England—he who needs no reminders; he asks for news of the primroses in the old woods, he speaks stammeringly of sweetwilliams in misty village gardens, of skylarks on the downs, of the friendly golden fogs of London, short days and early candletimes, and robins singing on Christmas Day.

THE STATES—III

I arrived in San Francisco alone on Christmas Eve with five dollars in my possession, knowing no-one. I went to a rather expensive hotel in Oakland. No hotel, bad or good, was, practically speaking, within my means, so I might as well choose a good one.

I remember that my first difficulty was the bed. There was, as I saw at a glance, no bed in my bedroom. I concealed my surprise—I have a horror of seeming insular. This was evidently a Californian peculiarity—bedless bedrooms—and I must make the best of it. I opened the wardrobe to hang up my hat, and the bed, which was one of those very patent labour-saving beds and had been trained to stand up on its hind legs in the wardrobe when not in use, unfolded with a crash on my head.

I did not feel financially justified in eating the hotel's Christmas dinner. So I bought some biscuits and a bar of chocolate and went out to the Golden Gate beach. There was a cold swift mist leaping to shore over the tall barrier of the wintry breaking waves. The sun was thickly wrapped away in dark red-grey clouds and the sands looked pink and more ethereal than the sky. Three dogs were very kind to me, teaching me to throw sticks into the sea in the San Francisco way. They and I sat wagging our tails in a cold but cheerful row, sharing biscuits (which they called crackers) and chocolate, and remembering other Christmases. A seagull joined us and proved to be a biscuit-maniac. It ate till it could hardly bend its neck. But when I gave it a piece of chocolate, its beak fell. A look of intense reproach came into its round eye; it hurried to the sea and spat the piece of chocolate into a retreating wave. It was too deeply offended to rejoin me and the dogs. But we didn't mind. All the more Christmas dinner for us....

THE STATES—IV

Being alive at all is an incessant shock and, I think, all the best lives are melodramas. Nevertheless in the course of every life the shock must hang fire at times. And in the construction of the melodrama there must be flaws, long-deferred entrances, maybe, on the part of the hero or heroine, or tardy exits on the part of the comic relief, or too much dialogue on the part of everybody. Moments between shocks are very hard moments to bear. To work one's way round the world is to be often gloriously surprised and often exquisitely uncertain and often futureless. But even so, there are moments when one is only too sure....

These lapses, I remember, seemed especially frequent in the life of an Editorial reader to a California publishing house which concentrated on scientific works. In California I tried to be a University coach, a lady's maid, a collector of overdue bills for an irascible firm, a salesman of boys' books—and, last of all, an Editorial reader. The last was the best-paid, the most comfortable, the most dignified—and the most dreadfully sure.... Or so it seems to me now. I remember reading a zoological book named, with extraordinary candour, the Boring Isopod. This Isopod, the author stated, could bore even rock and, personally, I can well believe it.

And, as it happened, my intimacy with the Isopod was interrupted by an earthquake. I had never experienced an earthquake before. I had always supposed that an earthquake was a weakness on the part of the earth, and that the feeling would be one of floppy giving way. On the contrary, the feeling was indescribably tense and energetic, as though the gods clenched their fists, as though titanic muscles were contracted suddenly. The office and the Boring Isopod and I were gripped, lifted, and let go. All the eucalyptus trees outside bowed and drew a hissing breath.

For several days the awakening shock of that earthquake stayed with me; the adventures of the Isopod sang themselves to me like a saga. Being alive was uncertain again. And when this feeling died away, having waited expectantly without result for a repetition of the helpful phenomenon, I took the matter into my own hands. I approached an aviator and, having pressed ten dollars into his hand, said, in effect, "Sir, be an earthquake to me." He replied, "T'ain't enough, ma-am. You can't get nothing worth-while for ten bucks...." Ten dollars, however, was all I had. I told him that I was a writer and would boost him to the best of my ability in return for a satisfactory shock. (And so I did. On my recommendation, probably hundreds of readers of the London *Star* made a note of the name of Roland S. Thomson.) He complied. In his company, mounted upon a Curtis biplane, I ricocheted from one pillar of the Golden Gate to the other, I turned upside down over San Francisco and saw the skyscrapers hanging like chandeliers over my head, I pounced upon cowering Alcatraz Island like a hawk upon a rabbit, and skipped facetiously over the whistling masts of ships. I was absolutely terrified.

At any rate I suggest these homely remedies for what they are worth, to a world surely suffering—at least in parts—from a very confusing lack of war. Earthquakes, to be sure, should be taken with care and cannot always be resorted to in moderation. But there is always a Roland S. Thomson available to everyone who possesses ten dollars and a select public. The only drawback is that one can only once enjoy a thing for the first time. Even a shock can become sure....

Still, a fertile mind will easily evolve equivalent forms of shock. If the worst comes to the worst, there is always the Electric Eel at the Zoo. I should like, by the way, to witness a meeting between the Electric Eel and the Boring Isopod.

THE STATES—V

"You're some stoodent," said the young doctor. "You've most always got a book in your hands. What's that—*Saturday Evening Post*? Dandy book that. I do a g'deal of reading myself."

"Aw Doc," said the bandaged girl in the next bed. "J'ever read the *Rosary*?"

"Sure I read it."

"Gee, what a book.... Gee, I cried till I was sick to me stomach.... Tck tck.... Poor guy went blind.... Gee, she was a peach ... disguised her voice an' all.... Tck tck.... You know, Doc, I guess I'm crazy, but it's a fact I take a book like that as much to heart as if it was reel life. You know what I mean, a reely *good* book like that. Gee, didn't seem like it was just made up. 'Member that Duchess ... and the mansion? That's what I call a reel *true* book...."

"You said it, lady," agreed the doctor, but I was the ward's prize stoodent and he turned again to me. "J'ever read a book called *Decameron* by a Wop? It's got more meat in it than most of the punk that a lotta white men write, let me tell you. Care to have me loan it you? Lotta women wouldn't stand for it, but you're a stoodent. Somebody told me you write books as well, is that so? Well, say, it's bin an interesting talk we had and—do you know what?—you've kinda inspired me to write a book myself.... Bin in my mind for years, but I've never gotten around to making a start. Yes, ma-am ... the subject'll be Cirrhosis of the Liver...."

JAPAN—I

Who was it who first sailed across the Pacific? I have an idea that it must have been Thomas Cook & Son because—(if I remember aright)—Thomas Cook discovered Australia and—probably—Son discovered New Zealand to match. Dear Thomas Cook ... his office is the world and somewhere in his ledgers, I know, lies hidden the secret of real adventure and of eternal youth. Look at Son, for instance. Ever since history began he has been as elusive as Love and has never yet made the mistake of achieving a name of his own or growing up. I may be wrong, but I imagine that Thomas Cook was among the first to evolve from slimy and primeval chaos and, directly he was dry, began distributing granite tickets for trips up newly arisen mountains. And when Son was born, he brought into the business that priceless asset which has been the essence of Thomas Cook's prosperity—the spirit of search for impossible things. When I think of Thomas Cook I am proud to be an Englishwoman, and when I think of Son I am proud to be a daughter.

Great as should be our admiration for people who go anywhere now for the first time, we should remember that at least they have newspapers to take off hats to them and say thank you. The original Tourist Fathers of blessed memory had, as a rule, nothing but a gratified conscience and a royal snub to look forward to.

After starting across the Pacific myself I found less difficulty than before in realising the intrepidity of those first travellers. I travelled in the smallest and dingiest Japanese passenger ship on the Pacific—yet I realise that its discomforts can be nothing to those surmounted by the first climbers up and down that mountainous swell. I imagine easily how those early great waves must have hungered for the bones of their first challengers. Even for my bones they hungered to such a degree that they broke one. By the time I had reached Honolulu I had actually a broken shoulder in addition to scores of minor wounds acquired by contact with walls, floors, funnels, masts, stewards, and any fellow-passengers harder in texture than myself. One wave actually threw someone else's fried egg and a carving knife at me along the whole length of a table.

The question of the food of the pioneering tourists is one which I can hardly bear to contemplate. A minor liner's food is like the conversation of some people I know; it starts with an almost hysterical brilliance; all treasures are produced extravagantly during the first outburst. And after that—corned beef ... canned tomatoes ... very weary eggs.... The eggs on board my ship were so tired that it was no surprise to me to find them one day posing on the menu as *Boiled Eggs à la Religieuse.* Nobody dared to eat them under this ominous name, but I understood, I sympathised, as I try to sympathise with all weary yearning souls. Indeed I thought the idea particularly beautiful.

Since therefore the Pacific—even to-day—is an ocean conspicuous for its lack of grocers, department stores, dairy-farms or other modern conveniences, my brain reels when I think of the tourists who travelled in a pre-canned-tomato age.

I should like to know what were the fears—probably courageously secret fears—felt by those first adventurers who did not even know the world was round and that—at any rate—Piccadilly Circus was always remotely ahead. Anything was possible in a world so inconceivable and so cruel. Myself, looking at that cynical sliding sea, I think I know what form my terrors would have taken. For at first the sea battled with us as though defying our challenge, and later it ran ahead of us, mocking us.... "Have your way then, fools, sail on, sail on ..." and last of all it was suddenly terribly smooth and terribly pale under a blind black sky. A great wind for a few hours beat the sea absolutely flat; here and there a few hairs of spray went up like steam. Behind the squealing of the wind we could hear the flaying rain and the sea hissing like an aroused dragon. And still the sea was level as the water of a great waterfall, just above the edge. And I know that—if I had been the first traveller—I should have been sure then that this was the great Edge of the World, and that over that edge the doomed taut sea and my little silly doomed ship would fall, shrieking, hissing down into a chaos of nethermost stars.

It was almost incredible to find that imagined terror past when the influence of the wind upon the sea made itself felt at last. The ship, no longer spellbound, swung and kicked healthily in a radiance of flying spray and stars and phosphorus.

Yet still, it seems, adventurers set sail to unknown ports. There was a man on our ship who turned aside on a new journey and will never come home to Japan now. He was Japanese, and he died in the steerage on New Year's Day while most of the crew and nearly all the passengers were dancing drunk. The sailors danced on the lower deck, singing high, metallic, unending, unbeginning songs, and beating their hands in time to their dancing. To this rather heartless sound the last sad adventurer began his new journey.

Next evening, as the moon dispersed the clouds accumulated by a stormy sunset, the body of the traveller, with leaden weights at his feet, was given a lonely farewell feast on the deck. A little table was spread with rice and fruit, and all the Japanese fellow-voyagers of this man who had no friends filed past his couch of honour one by one and saluted him. At a little distance a Portuguese priest, uninvited but kind, read the Christian burial service on the chance that a few stray blessings might thus be lured out of the generous moonlit spaces for the benefit of so forlorn a pilgrim. The moon, besides preparing for the traveller a white road up the sea, threw stars of silver broadcast on all the waves. These, I thought, must be the spirits of other men who had died at sea, assembling to show this newcomer the way. And indeed, as he slipped over the edge—over his ultimate edge—all the spirits gathered gladly round him and, as we left the place behind, we could still see a great starry crowd about it. I was glad that a good-bye so exquisite should have followed an end so noisy and so friendless. Only, when I saw Fuji standing on a cloud as we came into Yokohama, I was sorry that anyone who had loved that—as every Japanese loves Fuji—should die out of sight of it.

But Fuji, after all, is another story.

Japan is a fair story even the first word of which cannot be told by me. For I arrived in Yokohama with only about ten dollars plus a ticket to Hongkong. It was sleety midwinter in the height of the Spanish influenza epidemic and I had a broken shoulder.

To come, a woman alone, from California to Japan has the effect of a heavy fall. In California women, though not—as I think—essentially independent, are socially precious. In Japan they are trash. In California a woman becomes almost tired of being supported in and out of public vehicles as though she were fainting, of having kerbstones and puddles pointed out to her as though she were blind, and of having packages a few ounces in weight snatched away from her as though she had stolen them. In Japan, on the contrary, you may try—in spite of one arm in a sling—to carry two suit-cases and a typewriter at once, be swept into gutters by jinrickshas and at the same time be bitten by a horse with a straw petticoat and a red and yellow ornament on its spine but no manners—(Japanese horses dote on the flavour of women)—but no true Japanese will notice you or help you at all. Except that a policeman will probably choose that moment to ask you in Japanese for your passport or, failing that, for the date of your grandfather's first marriage and for your reason for being in existence. If, in reply, you winningly recite the two or three Japanese remarks you have learnt—a request for hot water or for another boiled egg—the policeman is not mollified but says, "No spik Inglis," and repeats his demands in a much fiercer voice. On the whole, in Japan you realise that you have committed such a social error in being born that you instinctively acquire the habit of apologising for being present or absent as the case may be, or for being trodden on or bitten or anything.

Once I committed half of a real crime, the other half being committed by another member of my condemned sex. She and I were passing the outer gate of the Mikado's palace in Tokyo when two motor-cyclists in uniform, riding furiously abreast, charged past us shouting something that we took to be merely the usual police maledictions. But they were followed by more loudly cursing outriders, and we then realised that we were sharing the responsibility for some unusually offensive crime. Turning to our ricksha-men to appeal for advice, we found that they had retreated to the side of the road and were there prostrating themselves reverently. The flaw in their patriotism, however, was the fact that they had left us in the middle of the road, rolled up in rugs in tilted rickshas, I helpless with horror, and my friend, with blasphemous gigglings.

I do not know who was the Japanese royalty who now began to pass us in several carriages and four; I only know that his progress was marred by the necessity of an unprincely detour, a slight but hideous bending in the august straight line of his route, to allow for the mushroom-like sprouting of two foreign females in derelict rickshas in his path. I am sure that only concern for dignity and the royal horses saved us from being driven over.

I went to a Geisha show in Yokohama with an Englishman. I went feeling like an empress because the show was called into being for my benefit; I came away feeling less than the dust. At the door of the house we were received—or rather my companion was received—by a flock of little twittering women who clustered round him, removed his shoes, and conveyed him affectionately into the house. He was treated by them exactly as a Californian woman is treated by men. They indicated to him the joints in the mats in case he should fall over them, and the ceiling in case he should knock his head against it. Now and then a new twitterer, after a profound reverence, joined his escort. As for me, I was left to remove my own shoes in the company of the ricksha coolies, and pant behind the procession, padding unloved on frozen feet. Finally we reached a room furnished exquisitely with emptiness. The walls, which were sliding screens, were of gold paper in black wooden frames; the handles by which the screens were moved were black silk tassels. There was nothing in the room but a bowl in a corner containing a gnarled dwarf cedar and another bowl in the middle containing glowing charcoal. The human inmates were decorative enough for any room. They were two little dancers, aged, as they indicated to us on their fingers, thirteen and fifteen years; their faces were very brilliantly and crudely painted; their hair was caught in wide black loops by vivid pins; their kimonos seemed to lack no possible colour; their obis were tied behind in puffed exaggerated bows, and each one carried a fan stuck in her obi over her heart. These two little flowers, like Moore's sunflower, turned their faces to one sun only. They settled my companion on a cushion embroidered with a pheasant, and brought in a low table beautified with delicate bowls of food to be placed before him. As an afterthought, and at my companion's request, they posed me on a lesser cushion embroidered with a mere frog. They danced for him. Their dancing was a sort of sleep-walking; their minds did not seem to take the slightest interest in what their feet and hands and delicate little bodies were doing; their cold small eyes looked out of their painted faces without inspiration or enthusiasm. Later they took a certain interest in me as though in a curious animal. They pulled my hair gently to see how it worked; they cooed with surprise while experimenting on it with Japanese pins—an experiment to which bobbed hair does not conveniently lend itself. They felt the materials of my clothes with industrious impersonal hands, untied my sling, opened my handbag and, finding a tobacco pouch and cigarette papers in its unladylike depths, demanded patronisingly to be shown how to roll.

I cannot help feeling glad that when my soul was, in the beginning, classified as female and given to an underling angel to be disposed of on earth, it was not fitted with a Japanese body. I cannot think that there would be very much left of that soul by now.

A Japanese husband, I am told, when introducing his wife to a man friend, says, in effect, "Sir, this is my little nuisance." The friend replies, "On the contrary, sir, she is more beautiful than a flower." The lady listens to this cancelling out of opinions; she bows humbly, but her eyes, I know, are cold and neutral. Her body bends; her hands serve always; her lips are ready with apology—and what more could any man desire?

While my money lasted, and on the proceeds of a couple of newspaper articles and an "Interview with Stella Benson", I managed to go to Kyoto and back. Almost my only happy moments in Japan were spent in the tangled shadows of trees and temples in Kyoto and during a day on Lake Biwa. We returned from Lake Biwa by an underground river, I remember, in the light of bland paper lanterns and to the sound of echoing chanteys from unseen singers hauling their way up against the splashing, tinkling, dimmed current.

I came back to Yokohama with my ticket to Hongkong as my only asset. I went to a Russian refugee hotel to await a ship and there was overcome by Spanish influenza. The rare persons who occasionally attended to me did so wearing masks like demon dogs. After a week I managed to reel on board a China-bound Japanese ship and there finished my attack in the orthodox way with the lung complications that were worn by the best people with influenza that year. If I had not clung with a desperate firmness to the brass rail of my bunk, I should have been repatriated at Kobe. But luckily a coal strike delayed us, so the quarantine officers allowed me to wait and see. Also someone had given me a little japonica tree in full flower and a tiny Japanese garden of old twisted trees and gaudy fairy bridges in a box—and these things always drew the attention of Japanese quarantine men away from me. A flower is a part of all the best business in hand in Japan—a much more important part than is a woman.

JAPAN—II

This is the story of a curious little conversation in the (late) Grand Hotel, Yokohama, with a kind, tipsy man whom I had met at a dance. During my last two days in Yokohama when I could just stand after my attack of influenza, he came and fetched me each afternoon in a ricksha from my miserable Russian hotel to sit in the Grand Hotel and sniff the perfume of cocktails and health and wealth. My arm was still in a sling, my face no doubt a hollow and ashy green and, as the sun went down, caution prompted me to get home to bed before the chill of night began.

"Sit still," he said. "Yes, I know it's seven o'clock, but I'm not going to let you go home. I want to save you. Do you really think I don't know what's the matter with you? Do you really imagine you can go about with your arm in a sling and your face that colour and your determination to get away by yourself at a fixed time every afternoon— and continue to hide from your friends what you're suffering from?... My dear, morphia's an enemy that speaks for itself. Now, now, nothing you can say can deceive me—you see I know that protests are symptoms in themselves.... My dear girl, you needn't be afraid of me, I've known drug-takers before. I loved one.... I spent all my fortune in trying to save her and at last, on a doctor's advice, I sent her home.... Well ... she drowned herself from the ship.... For her sake, you must let me help you...."

The story of his love was, I happen to know, completely untrue. It was part of the damask of romantic fiction with which he covered his purposeless and fuddled life. I never saw him entirely sober or entirely unromantic. But all his fictions were kind and dealt with kindness. He was killed in the Club bar in the Yokohama earthquake, and I am sure that death interrupted him in one of the gentle rambling lies he so often told about the ideal life that he had never achieved. I hope he had a rapt sentimental listener for his last lie. He was almost always just sober enough to feel the need of that.

MANILA—MACAO— HONGKONG

There are three ways of occupying an alien place—first, to absorb; second, to be absorbed; third, neither to absorb nor to be absorbed.

Manila is a vessel filled with oil and water. The Filipinos remain extremely Filipino. As for the Americans—100 per cent is a figure that admits of no modification.

Manila has a sort of illusion of siege attached to it. The camp of America is pitched outside the confident sunny walls of the old city. The traveller first sets foot in a raw impermanent-looking area and could for a while believe himself in some Middle Western township. You may see a bald red trail labelled Twenty-Somethingth Street. You almost expect to see the sign so expressive of the glowing Western spirit—DRIVE SLOWLY, CONGESTED BUSINESS DISTRICT— erected hopefully in a wilderness of scrub and sand. The traveller toils across acres of imported America towards the hotel which rears itself, indecently opulent, above a waste of junk and lumber yards and grey hot grass—and suddenly, like the first pioneers in California, he meets the challenge of the old world again across the desert—here is Spain again, Manila, girdled with her golden wall and crowned with a romantic sun.

Americans and Filipinos, as it seemed to me, live together in 50 per cent liberty, 49 per cent equality and 1 per cent fraternity. Politically, a great deal is said about brotherhood—personally, almost nothing.

I arrived in Manila during the Carnival. But the buildings erected for the occasion had been burnt down the night before my arrival. Merry-makers were pathetically trying to make merry in the smoke among the ashes. I do not know what a raw or uncooked carnival in

Manila may be like, but this one which had been "tried in the fire" was literally refined by the process. I was astonished at the self-conscious politeness of the occasion; an atmosphere of I-can't-talk-to-you-we-haven't-been-introduced prevailed. People went laboriously masked and dominoed in select and well-chaperoned parties; it seemed that men poured confetti with feverish caution over their aunts and sisters. Groups of virtuous business men and their overstitched wives stood watching through shocked pince-nez a handful of young new Sammies who were making so bold as to dance with some pretty Filipino girls. The girls wore their national dress—wired gauze at the shoulders, high Elizabethan ruff behind the head, looped complicated skirt. The Americans wore their national dress....

As for Hongkong, that grave and misty tilted island, it makes no claim at all to a spirit of equality. It is a solid lump of England; from waterside to peak-tip the little funicular carries Anglo-Saxon civilisation up and down. The average Hongkonger has a tendency to address all Chinese in a throaty tone of authority as "Boy". He is quite sure that to show respect to "these natives" "lowers British prestige". So Chinese Hongkong has acquired a soul that only answers to the name of Boy. Only the congested attached city of junks and sampans, moored and swinging with the tides at the island's edge, is true to its own vivid and insanitary convictions. Little red and gold paper prayers flutter at every vessel's mast and stern to protect the water city from the march of civilisation.

The city of Macao is old, but it seems older than its years. Here, I think, you have China victorious. Portugal lies drugged and asleep in the arms of China.

The empty shell of Portuguese taste is there, the coloured plaster walls, the low corrugated red tile roofs, the quiet gardened convents, the churches full of a vulgar and ardent daylight.... Yet the city seems to me almost wholly Chinese at heart. The broad calm masks of Chinese women look down on the streets through carved bars and trellises that seem made to frame much more radiant faces; the blunt eccentric shapes of papayas and bananas fill the squares and gardens instead of roses and olives; the churches are deserted except for a few little tranquil Chinese matrons, trousered and sleek, with their babies strapped in big coloured handkerchiefs on to their shoulders. And fire, born of a Chinese sun, has devoured the cathedral, except for its façade which stands stark and stricken, with sunny space as much behind it as before. But the Chinese temples stand, their ferocious porcelain sky-lines bristling with dragons and dolphins, their dusty and slovenly altars presided over by absent-minded but complacent Buddhas. And the Chinese fan-tan dens stand—are encouraged by the Portuguese Government—and there you can go and take rather monotonous risks with a spare dollar and watch the Chinaman as he best loves to be—with his head bent over a board on which all that he has lies in danger.... Only when the shadows of the big African soldiers cross the door does it seem as if Portugal opened an indolent eye.

HONGKONG

Whenever I go to Hongkong now, tall fashionable young Chinese and Eurasians lean across chemists' counters, hurry out of garages and bound into my cabin in the guise of hotel touts—to remind me that once I taught them certain branches of scholastic knowledge. Both they and I forget now—and perhaps never knew—exactly what knowledge they succeeded in acquiring from me. In the days when I was working my way round the world I thought myself lucky to be engaged to teach a class of fifty boys in all branches of human knowledge—(except mathematics)—for a hundred and forty Hongkong dollars a month.

I lacked not only degrees, diplomas and all necessary knowledge, but also the voice and address of the teacher. I had a very noisy and robust-spirited class, but to its credit let me say that no boy ever actually defied me. If any boy had defied me on a hot day I should have cried; I don't mind confessing that now. The boys, in spite of a penchant for pea-shooters and cribs, were in the main extremely kind to me, and I think that was because my teaching did not tax their brains, and my discipline was so erratic that it demanded an almost paternal tolerance on their part. The ages of my boys ranged from ten or so—in the Eurasian half of the class—to twenty-three—in the Chinese benches—but all alike were strangely soothed by my "method". I treated them exactly like a kindergarten. A lesson in hygiene, for instance, would be accompanied—and, I firmly maintain, enlivened—by sketches on the blackboard representing such subjects as a microbe—in a facetious top-hat—carrying a little portmanteau labelled Typhoid, tripping up over a Smell called Permanganate of Potash. History and Scripture also lent themselves to illustration. I am sure that these "twopence-coloured" lessons dwelt in inattentive Chinese minds more surely than did the "penny-plain" of some of the more experienced teachers.

Scripture was my worst difficulty since, to my generation, I think, the Bible is rather a sentiment than a conviction. Most of the stories are hard to teach—from the school point of view—as *true*, and still harder to show from my own point of view as the wild and lovely things they are to me. It is difficult to look on our old-remembered and insidious Bible as a new and sudden study, in any case. And it is difficult to cope conscientiously with the response of fifty sceptics to Western "superstitions". Legend is a thing that the carriers of Western civilisation have carefully drilled the Chinese to view with suspicion in their own history and lore. Such a message, once preached, can never be unsaid. Such a serpent, loosed in the garden of lovely and unlikely and half-forgotten things, turns upon the hand that freed it.

"But that only superstition, marm, didn't it?" Such a fire can dry up the watery triumphs of Noah, and, in the clear light of that fire, all glories and stories—the angelic checking of Abraham's fanatic knife above the neck of little Isaac; the excellent close bargaining with God for the preservation of Sodom and Gomorrah; David's schoolboy victory over Goliath; the business successes of the dreamer, Joseph, and the poetry that intruded into the efforts of prosy Moses—all these look cold and lifeless.

"Superstition ... no ... yes ... but anyway beautiful and amusing.... Well, I'll show you how David looked, perhaps, saying good-bye to his few sheep in the wilderness...."

The blackboard, a bridge between fact and fancy, was our refuge.

When I first mentioned to my class that I wanted to be in my turn instructed in the ways of Chinese restaurants and Chinese theatres, there was a sound of reproach in fifty voices.

"Oh no, marm, you didn't could like such thing. Chinese theatre too much superstitions...."

I had to assert my authority, such as it was, and finally Ng Poon Wong, a hitherto care-free creature, the noisiest and most intelligent in the class, undertook the dreadful duty of bear-leader. There were two bears to be led, myself and an enquiring sailor. About one-tenth of one per cent of the personnel of the British Navy is occasionally willing to Lower the British Prestige to this extent, if I may say so without shattering England's faith in her floating bulwark.

Ng Poon Wong ordered us a dinner. Scarlet with embarrassment at our conspicuous gaucherie, he watched us knock pigeon's eggs on to the floor with chopsticks, he watched us dip each mouthful into all the

28

wrong little condiment-saucers, he bowed sadly to us as we drank his health in a blend of methylated spirit and cheap scent. And, being Chinese, he kept his word under difficulties—he took us to the theatre.

We were the only occidentals there. Next to me sat a contemptuous Chinese duke (or something) with a little skull-cap and a fine brocade robe which he drew away from accidental contact with my vulgar taffeta. The third and fourth fingers of his left hand wore fingernails longer than the fingers themselves, yet, although much hampered by this aristocratic disability, the martyr took snuff without ceasing out of a little jade bottle with a coral stopper. Up and down all the aisles of the theatre walked men with little towels in cauldrons of hot water. On being signalled to by members of the audience, these men threw the steaming screwed-up towels over scores of heads with perfect aim. The recipient of a towel wiped his face, his shaven head, his naked breast and his arms with it and then, with strength renewed, flung it back to the cauldron to be re-soaked and used again. I watched fascinated, trembling for my own hat, but I never saw an accident in this towel air-service.

Above us the gallery was fringed with the soles of the bare feet of the more plebeian audience; scantily dressed vendors of sunflower seeds pushed about among our knees; the arm between each two chairs was flattened to form a little table on which constantly replenished cups of leafy tea were balanced by kind but dangerous men who swung spitting boiling kettles about with loud shouts that drowned the drama. Indeed the drama seemed to be the last thing considered in a Chinese theatre.

Of the large stage, about one-twentieth was reserved for the performers. Right centre, the troupe's washing was being hung out by a large and voluble company of *amahs* to drip upon the actors' heads. Left centre, half-a-dozen supers undressed suddenly and went to bed. Two little boys raced on scooters up and down the back of the stage. All the members of the cast who were not at the moment acting stood about on the stage dressing desultorily, discussing the weather prospects or the price of rice with the orchestra or with members of the audience at the back of the hall.

The orchestra itself seemed bewilderingly telescopic; at one moment it would consist of at least four gongists, six tea-trayists, two bagpipers without the bags, and a dozen flautists, all playing industriously without reference to one another or to any score. At another moment half the performers—or sometimes all but one—perhaps in

29

the middle of a top note by the hero, would suddenly go away to have a drink. The hero, looking only slightly silly, after a surreptitious reproachful glance at the empty orchestra benches, would finish his song bravely alone. There was a jazz man, however, who played about ten instruments at once with different toes, fingers, elbows and knees. He remained faithful throughout, apparently because he was playing in his sleep.

In front of the orchestra were three chairs. Sometimes these, according to Ng Poon Wong, represented mountains, sometimes a double bed, sometimes a sacred grove of bamboos, sometimes the Emperor's palace, and then again, sometimes they were unexpectedly admitted to be three chairs and people actually sat on them. Between these versatile chairs and what might have been the footlights—only there were no footlights—a space of about ten feet by six was sacred to about six actors and about twelve property men.

The property men seemed to find the actors very much in their way. Ng Poon Wong told us that they were invisible—"You don't can see all those helping man"—and we were glad to know this for, had we believed the evidence of our own eyes, we should have thought the useful fellows rather inadequately dressed for classical drama. In spite of their negligent look, however, they kept the drama together. They bristled with little tickets describing the varying rôles of the three chairs; whenever an actor wanted to die or to kneel before a superior, the nearest property man produced a little mat; whenever anyone started on a journey—sometimes as many as seven times round the chairs or, on one occasion, up one end of the row of chairs and down the other—a property man stuck a large pointed hat upon the traveller's passive head. The property men kept the actors supplied with horses or, in other words, little bamboos decorated with red tassels, which were stage shorthand for horses. Directly a mandarin was given one of these, his legs began to frisk about of their own volition, so to speak, leaving his dignified upper manners unimpaired—and the most incurable occidental could then see that he was mounted.

As for the story, it was an edifying one about a man who was almost too faithful to his grandmother. His life's work, as he saw it, was seeking bamboo shoots for the old lady's table. The emperor sent files of emissaries round and round the chairs to summon the hero to a high position at court, but the filial creature would not go. At one time a demon tried to tempt him—but here the action became too frank for comment; suffice it to say that the demon was a lady and that Ng Poon

30

Wong chose this moment to begin explanations. "She want marriage ..." he said, but I fancy this was an overstatement. Even this danger the hero escaped. Finally the grandmother herself, not in the least grateful for this fidelity, tired of bamboo shoots and probably thinking only of the separation allowance, insisted on her descendant's acceptance of a well-paid job at a great distance. So the poor fellow span three times round in agony, seized a horse from a property man, who was scratching his head with it, and rode away with an aggrieved *frou-frou* of silk petticoats.

All the actors were men but, whether they were enacting men or women, they all chanted their parts in strained falsetto voices. They were at first stiffly encrusted in gorgeously embroidered robes, but, as the evening wore on and became hotter, these robes became unpractical. By the end of the play most of the performers were naked down to their middles, except for decent cascades of false beard and false hair. Property men came with hot towels and scrubbed each artist down back and front at intervals, without, of course, interrupting the action. Every actor carried his discarded robes on his arm, to remind us that he still possessed them.

The performance closed with a fighting ballet. A very nimbly jumping person wearing the mask of an ape, and another, rather less athletic, dressed as a tiger, each with followers to match, fought intricate and ingenious battles, jumping under and over one another, clashing weapons in rhythm and chiming challenge with challenge, following accurate figures that suggested sanguinary country dances. After an hour or two of this we left the performance still closing, and no doubt it continued to close for the rest of the night. The gongists and the tenor and alto tea-trays were just settling down to their work, the flautists had been out-crashed. It seemed there never was a night so silent as the night that greeted us outside with a kind winking of stars entangled with the climbing lights of men; never was a sound so blessedly little as the sound of the bare running feet of the ricksha men and the lapping of the moonlit water under the broad sleeping cities of sampans and junks moored along the wharfside.

THE LITTLE JOURNEY

It was morning when the ship slid out from under the eaves of Hongkong. Hongkong is like the great shadow of a Chinese temple upon the sky; its summit is nearly always ruled straight by a high horizontal cloud, its slopes have the optimistic concavity of temples and only lack a titanic dragon and a curled lion or two to make the temple suggestion complete. At night, so absurdly is Hongkong tilted, it loses its outline; the lights of the Peak climb so high and the stars so low.

But it was morning when my little ship deftly extricated herself from the tangle of shadows and ships in the harbour. Between the tawny junks, the low grey battleships with decks like petrified forests, the dark rusty tramp steamers, the hooded sampans on which the Chinese water-coolies with their women and babies and cats and flowers live—between this and that my little ship picked her way.

My fifty Chinese boys in three motor launches had come, partly to wish me well and partly for the pleasure of disobeying orders. In a cloud of white pyjama-ed boys, I had alighted on the surprised little ship and now—Good-bye ... good-bye ... good-bye.... I could hardly see them, so furiously did they urge their purring boats—each boat the tip of a feathered arrow of spray—in figure eights about the slow course of my *Chang-Shing*. I saw them at last like little frantic water-beetles beneath the upraised heel of tall Hongkong.

And at last Hongkong itself was dim, and the crystallised beads and loops of silver cloud blew across the great harbour and obscured the faces of the gaunt hills of the New Territory.

When Hongkong slipped over the grey-glass rim of the sea, the *Chang-Shing* seemed all alone like a guest at a strange deserted feast. A great company of remote islands stood about her and, without welcome, watched her pass. I have never been so much alone on a ship before; the ways of globe-trotters have been too much my ways; men and women have been between me and the sea. I have criminally associated ships with little sentimental affairs, with the autobiographies of travelling salesmen, with thwarted Grand Slams in No Trumps, with beef tea and cheap scent. The *Chang-Shing* carried only indigo and—by courtesy—me. She was only smart in comparison with some of the junks. And, perhaps in order to show herself to advantage, for the first two days of her voyage north she rolled, snorting proudly, up the rough ruts of a plunging avenue of junks. Chinese fishing junks are like skeletons in crinolines. Their tattered matting sails, like fans, are stiffened with bamboos; wreathed about their figures are red paper prayers, fluttering to catch the attention of the heedless gods. Often these junks are tilted forward, stern high and bows awash, as though they contemplated diving. They swung at anchor, jealously guarding their little claims in the sea, each claim staked out by a hedge of flagged bamboos floating upright.

China, with hills dull red or dunes bleakly white, ran by us to the west. There was never a sign of life on the coast and, at night, never a light. We passed a lighthouse on the third day; white and sophisticated, it sprang up in a lonely dream-bound world. A man waved from it. Could he be a man and not a god? How terribly the sea must count to him....

"You an' him can have the sea for me," said the skipper who was from Dundee and, like most sailors, believed that he wanted to settle down. He said rather prettily that all he would want to see of the sea for the rest of his life would be a "wee far seelver edge...." He talked little of the immediate sea; his stories, which held me spellbound over a lingering mango or lichee in the tiny saloon, dealt with adventures more or less amphibious—tigers in the South China hills, quarrels and hot nights in Indian ports, mine-laying in the North Sea in war-time, the pursuit of gold in Australia by one Weather-r-rbeaten Br-r-rown, the occasional illicit relief of Port Arthur during the Russo-Japanese War, the first voyage of an apprentice round the world in a sailing ship thirty years ago. Sometimes the talk turned on typhoons and pirates, but these things are so common they rarely produce a new yarn. Every island talks of one typhoon until the next stops the talk; every river mouth echoes with the monotonous doings of pirates. One of the most powerful trade unions in China, that land of perfect trade unions, is the pirates' guild, they say. Most of all, the skipper and the mate and, on occasions, the pilot and the firm's agent, loved to tell very small vague stories about other sailors—stories which everyone but the land-lubber

33

knew. Their minds were a network of names. "Then there was McKay—d'you mind what his bride said when he found her mither in the lair-rder? And Guthrie who called for carrots—in Shanghai ... and what was the tale of Fair-r-rguson an' the centipede?" One never appreciates the greatness of Scotland until one goes to sea.

The *Chang-Shing* dared not touch at so sophisticated a port as Shanghai, but one evening at sunset, on a sea of glazed crimson, she passed the mouth of the Yang-tse river. The perspective of the clouds followed that of the river, and there was a great feather of wine-coloured cloud rooted, as it seemed, in the sun itself; the tip of the plume hung low over our mast. The river withdrew into a low confusion of hills, and into that confusion the sun sank down alive.

We ran into a fog that night and the *Chang-Shing* rent her soul and mine with cries of warning to an apparently empty world. But the fog was like the curtain between two acts, for when at noon next day we shook ourselves clear of it we were in northern seas and the great square-sailed junks that travelled across our sight were of a new and more austere shape. The coast was clearer, fiercer and more scarred. Wei-hai-wei broke the outline of the cliffs and we could see the bulls of the British herd at rest—the dark formidable outlines of the China Squadron—and a mother-ship of submarines with her frolicsome young. And at Wei-hai-wei, though we did not put into harbour, a large number of passengers alighted. They were courtesy passengers like me, a great company of the most incorrigible land-lubbers, most unsuitably dressed for a sea voyage. Finches, jays, pigeons, little tentative flautists nameless to me, smooth grey-crested dandies with scarlet throats, a couple of sparrowhawks—lion and lamb alike, they had been sitting for the last twenty-four hours in agitated rows upon our rigging. They trusted me to a certain extent, though not to the point of eating crumbs which I spread out for them. They combed the deck for worms all round my chair. The sea-gulls laughed raucous nautical laughter at this innocent invasion. But the passengers knew what they were about. As one bird they disembarked at Wei-hai-wei.

We reached the port of Chefoo late on our sixth night. All next day, while coolies, dyed bright blue with indigo, piled into lighters the oozing sacks of our cargo, the skipper and I explored the sunstricken sordid city of Chefoo. It seemed to me—after Hongkong—a city baked and caked in squalor. The men beat the ponies, the boys beat the dogs, the babies tortured the lizards. The streets seemed full of dark men with faces contorted with anger and bodies full of the power of making anger felt. The churches—of which there were plenty—looked on decorously, feeling, no doubt, that here was copy for endless sermons.

The Yellow Sea is really very yellow, as yellow as a desert. Junks looked as though they had lost their way and run aground.

A pilot, full of wheezy jokes, came on board and inserted the *Chang-Shing* into the Pei-ho river. Two Chinese mud-forts, proved futile by naval guns in the Boxer rising, still keep up the pretence of guarding that narrow mouth. The *Chang-Shing* ignored them and began feeling her way up a waterway which is like a puzzle founded on a tireless repetition of the last letter of the alphabet. The earth was no less golden than the sea; the world, cupped in a glittering pale horizon, was like an orgy of golden wine. Villages were built of yellow earth; even shadows were yellow; there was no colour but yellow in the eyeless streets of the softly-moulded villages. There were graves everywhere, cones of yellow mud varying in height and perfection of symmetry according to the importance of the occupant. It is a promotion to be dead in China, but the choice between a crumbling mud-house and a crumbling mud grave is a very small choice. The cities of the living and the cities of the dead are not divided. Movement in the land was chiefly provided by the salt-mills; like merry-go-rounds at a home fair they span and span, lacking only music and gaudiness and laughter. Sometimes mud-caked babies ran across a mud-beach to throw themselves down in the golden wave caused by the *Chang-Shing's* passing. In that wave the moored fishing-boats stirred uneasily; they were like dragonflies asleep; their nets were stretched on quivering bamboos at the tops of hinged masts.

Once, as the fringes of the smoke that overhangs Tientsin began to shut out the sun, there was music beside us and I looked down into a fishing-boat on its way home from sea. In the bows sat the musician, singing softly and vagrantly to a long-necked guitar; in the stern his partner had unbraided his waist-long, blue-black hair and combed it slowly with luxurious fingers. A tawny little boy in a single blue garment propelled the unhurried boat in time to the song. And then the city and the end of the journey invaded us.

PEKING—I

Until I went to Peking and met the Chinese dragon, I never cared for curly-haired heroes. I always thought them artificial. But the dragon, you can see, hasn't a spark of artifice about him; there is sincerity in every curl of him. Probably he tries hard to grease the kink out of his hair, to the secret regret of his mother. But there is nothing superficial about that kink—the ineradicable tendency comes out even in his marcelled spine.

I always liked lizards, and now I have transferred my more mature affections to dragons. I cannot determine exactly what the popular feeling in China towards dragons is. I cannot guess off-hand what sort of reception would be accorded a dragon who suddenly walked in by the Hatamen Gate and, after calling at the Legations as a gentleman should, went to cool off in the moat that surrounds the Forbidden City—that moat in which the little yellow glazed dragons that fortify the sky-line are reflected among the pink and white floating lotuses. I do not suppose that the Peking camels would shy so whole-heartedly at such a visitor as they do at a simple Ford car.

Sometimes you do meet a dragon in the street, walking vicariously on the legs of dozens of little boys. It has a band in front of it consisting of a few trays and a bass wheeze, so you can see that it has admirers and that they do their best to give it pleasure. Yet this dragon always looks to me thirsty and dissatisfied. Its tongue hangs out. I always used to attribute this to the music, but now I am informed that the purpose of this procession is to lure dilatory rain out of the sky.

But I repeat that if you are a dragon you cannot count on public opinion in China, even if you walk occasionally not without honour and have pom-poms stuck into your hide by means of toothpicks. Only the other century, the Chinese authorities found a stray dragon about ten miles out of Peking. They probably charged it with being without visible means of subsistence, but really they suspected it of world-swallowing—a vice peculiar to dragons. A dragon that has acquired the taste for worlds—like a sheep-dog that has started eating sheep—can never be cured. This particular dragon was caught practically red-handed. So the authorities came up behind it while it was asleep and built a big pagoda on its head and a little pagoda on its tail and so pinned it down. They did not try the well-precedented pinch of salt on the tail—the Chinese are a cautious race.

I go and look at that dragon sometimes. The coarse grass grows up his steep breast now, his profile is lost in granite boulders; twisted and crouching pines with silver trunks cling to his ribs. But still authority does not trust him, still the two heavy pagodas hold him down, and their bells, swinging in the wind, invoke the aid of heaven in a good work. And I admit that he is obviously not to be trusted. I know that he lies awake all day and all night, a prisoner forever, thinking of the worlds he hunted and of the worlds he caught.

I have a picture, embroidered in silk, that shows me the dragon when he was young. He is curly and lithe and metallic and he hunts a gold world across black space. Gold is always the colour of worlds on the wing; we all know that after we have hunted and caught one or two. But the dragon never learned much; he never knew why a thing that is gold when hunted should be ashes when caught. My silken picture shows him hollow-eyed and starved, dizzy with the spinning and splendour of untasted worlds. So he was caught and there he lies. The gentle weeds grow over his eyes and it is as well perhaps that he cannot see what I can see to-day—the great opalescent bubble of temptation blown anew every spring. He cannot see the banners of springtime in the great valley or the golden shining of the far roofs of the Forbidden City.

There he lies, bewildered, with cold ashes on his tongue. And he wonders where the goodness of good hunting goes, and whether hunting disappointment is better than not hunting at all.

PEKING—II

"Business as Usual", the inspiring Anglo-Saxon war-cry, obtains. I sit in my hospital office in Peking—in my capacity of X-ray assistant—side by side with a skeleton, and try to keep as cool as the skeleton looks, in a temperature of 106, and listen, with the characteristically subtle expression of the ignorant, to incoming rumours of war.

Everything connected with the great half-built American hospital for which I work is now decorated with the Stars and Stripes for moral protection. The primitive carts carrying out earth from our excavations to the outskirts of the city fly Old Glory from their mules' collars, to prevent either army from commandeering them. The earth-stained, thin-queued men on their shafts look upon themselves now as American citizens; they wave to us like brothers as we heave by in flagged rickshas. So ubiquitous is Martha Washington's design in flags up our *hutung* just now that, beginning to feel that I was remaining safe by means of false pretences, I bought a very small Union Jack. This I tied to the finger-nail of the dragon over our gate, to suggest to any loot-seeking band that might pass that the British Lion also had a paw in the matter.

I have one dread, and that is to see the Forbidden City at the mercy of shell-fire. The property brought by Chinese neighbours to us for protection is mostly tawdry and poor, but I think I shall gather the yellow and blue palaces and the rose-red walls and the dragony watch-houses and the great tented gates and the lotuses together and carry them home reverently to keep in a scented and sunlit place till the danger is over.

I write this in a temple outside a western gate where my English host and hostess live in great friendliness with priests and in the sound of the hoarse low temple bells. And as I write we are undergoing a call from the Chinese colonel of the barracks opposite. Behind his fan he talks urgently, and here and there wisps of the conversation are translated for me. He has no heart for war—there is, indeed, no heart and no sentiment in this war at all—at least for subordinates. There is no patriotism involved, and it is difficult to risk one's life with enthusiasm in a political quarrel the solution of which can bring no peace. The colonel's outlook is detached. The rebel, he says, is the better man in this war. There is no question of loyalty, for neither combatant is on poor China's side. Indeed to the impartial eye both factions seem to be in the position of rebels. One rebel, however, is countenanced—though unwillingly—by Government authority, and the other is not. The uncountenanced is the finer spirit, one gathers. Uncountenanced rebels generally are, I think.

PEKING—III

The war round Peking, which has been theoretically raging for some weeks, has become more prominent. In fact I have stumbled over the thing and barked my shins, or, in other words, caught a cold by fleeing in the middle of the night from an army.

After communications with the outer world had been cut last week and newspapers had petered out, we men-in-the-street of Peking rather lost touch with the war. We heard hourly that someone was running away from someone else, often that everyone was running away from everyone else in all directions. Sometimes Tuan Chi Jui was pursuing Wu Pei Fu in the direction of Tibet with every hope of getting there, as it seemed, and sometimes Wu Pei Fu was spilling Tuan Chi Jui over the coast into the Yellow Sea. We became quite callous about the war. It seemed, to say the least of it, childish for two armies large enough to know better to run about so quickly in such hot weather.

So, in the afternoon of a very hot day, after the word had been given—as afterwards appeared—to shut the city gates, I travelled, all unaware, in a ricksha to a friend's temple about five miles towards the Western hills. Nor did I know anything more—as romantic novelists say—except how red was the sunset on the red thirsty fields, and how kindly the stars looked down among the temple goldfish through the leaves of the scarlet-flowered creeper that drapes a great tree in the courtyard. I knew nothing more until two o'clock in the small hours, when we all awoke to find ourselves in the act of being rescued by a gallant compatriot in a Ford car. Tuan's army, it appeared, nimble as usual, was now running in a disorderly mood in our direction.

Our rescuer had spent three hours fawning upon the city gates, trying to find a sesame that would open them and allow him to come out and warn us. Finally the officer in charge, wearied by seeing the blunt obstinate nose of the Ford pressed against his gate, let out the rescuer on condition that he return within the hour or else forever hold his peace.

Our dressing was much sooner done than said, and a band of fugitives, eight strong, squeezed into the Ford four-seater. I sat on the folded canvas hood at the back and I saw a hedgehog cross the road but not a single army running in any direction whatever.

Each of Peking's gates is done in duplicate, so to speak; there is an inner and an outer gate. The outer gate that night looked austere and beautiful in the dark socket of its archway in the great wall. The gate was a dim Chinese red, and it was studded with bolts and big nails. There was no guard outside, no greeting but the gate itself, and that was like a final and absolute No. Our red-plumed Legation servant, who had been clinging to the mudguard throughout, wailed through the crack of the gate. Far away, from inside the inner gate, the guard replied in two snorts and a hiccough, which, being interpreted, meant, it appeared, that the gate was closed for the duration of war. The importunate Ford turned its bright embarrassing eyes on the gate and tooted in the starlight while Chinese repartee flickered up and down through the crack. And at last we could see all at once that the crack was wider, and then a soldier's face over a blank-shining paper lantern appeared in the opening.

So we got back into Peking.

I had only two regrets at the time—first, that we had left my friends' dog—a most charming Eurasian—and their parrot at the mercy of looters, and second, that we ran over a Chinese dog on the way in.

The army fulfilled expectations and reached our village that morning. I wonder what the parrot said.

Those were my only two regrets at the time, but next day I had many more, for the wounded arrived in our hospital. All day there were limp still figures on stretchers outside our X-ray room, waiting for examination.

I sat in the dark room under a spark of red light, taking notes of the position of the bullets as the examining doctor announced them. Some of the soldiers groaned like wild beasts, some never opened their eyes, some chattered hysterically to the attendants about their experiences, some cried when they saw the inexplicable apparatus or when the great screen slid down as though to crush them, some indicated their wounds with their beautiful thin fawn-coloured hands—as though their

41

wounds were not visible enough. They seemed so detached and so entirely without niches in the world, so aloof from one another, so much like hurt animals, that it seemed almost strange that they should have names to file and should remember their own ages. They were like ghosts passing through the flushed twilight of the X-ray room; they seemed to have no past and no future. They were the ruins of a lost army, their leader had forgotten them. Rumour had it that their general, escaping on an engine from the scene of his failure, had driven right through his army, over the living bodies of those who had failed with him. Many of them had lost their youth and their future in his service—but failure has no friends.

Collectively, experience seems to teach them nothing, and though these have fallen and been forsaken, others fight on, for no ideal, for no cause, for no reward, for no reason.

PEKING—IV

I was riding home towards Peking under the eaves of the outer wall of the Temple of Heaven. Peking is a maze of walls. The Chinese mind loves walls. A truly chaste Chinese village, however small, counts itself undressed without a high wall buttoned up to the neck.

In the space before the opposite wall of the Temple of Agriculture, a great crowd had built itself into an amphitheatre about a clear level place.

"What thing b'long there?" I asked the *mafu*.

"B'long number one piecee look-see," instantly replied the *mafu*, who is an optimist. Anything that several thousands of his fellow-countrymen were coming to see must be a number one look-see. So we stood waiting for the show until the *mafu*, having made enquiries, announced with increasing satisfaction, "Bimeby wantchee makee dead five piecee man."

Every face I could see at once seemed to me hideous, every smile fiendish. I set Woodrow, my pony, to try and struggle against the crowd towards the Chienmen gate which reared its guard-house safe and sun-tiled at the end of a long seething perspective. But the current was massively contrary to my course; there was a slow glacier of humanity coming and coming to see the show. An eager turbulence was abroad, the crowd, in comparison with the ordinary Chinese crowd, was rough; a series of jovial spirits thought fit to tease and strike Woodrow as we waded through, making him plunge and protest. Our flight was therefore very slow, and it seemed a long time before I could even pretend that I was out of sight of that ominous cleared space, bare except for a squad of Chinese soldiers waiting for their work and a line of American soldiers waiting for their amusement.

Presently along the broad road from Chienmen a growing growl of angry voices came to us. And then soldiers appeared, clearing a path through the crowd. The faces of the soldiers were convulsed with anger and effort; with the butts of their rifles they were hitting the heads and shoulders of the packed mass of men and women in front of them. Woodrow and I were carried away by an eddy in the crowd almost into a booth at the side of the street.

A passage was cleared, and five mule-drawn carts came along the passage. They were the same kind of carts as those that carry rubbish away from the city's activities to oblivion. The drivers, crouched on the shafts, had no light of interest in their eyes. On each cart there were four sullen-looking soldiers, and one condemned man with his arms and knees bound.

The first was either drunk or in an ecstasy of bravado: his head hung back, swinging from side to side, his eyes were tightly shut and he was singing in a piercing cracking voice that sometimes became a scream. The other four victims were fixed in various attitudes of terror and hopelessness. The third had his head bowed between his tense knees and, as he passed, the anger of the crowd found suddenly increased voice. A hoarse and sickening unison of reviling filled the air and seemed to rebound from side to side of the street. Whatever those poor thin half-paralysed boys had done, the crowd, in so lifting up its voice, hideously overstated its grievance. Even the action that followed the roar—an attempt on the part of men in the crowd to break through the guard and reach the prisoners—seemed more healthy than that horribly unanimous cursing.

The five carts went by. A sixth cart carried most suggestive properties for the show.

And then came a line of Ford cars, spruce and eager and exasperating as insects, filled with American and English men and women who had at last found something in Peking interesting enough to draw them away from the little tables in the hotel lounges. And the nearer I came to the city gate, the more swiftly did the crowd pass, hustling in rickshas, heaving in blue-hooded Peking carts, running on foot—running—running—running—dragging its faltering babies, urging its crippled pin-footed mothers and sisters, beating its donkeys, straining, cursing, all for fear lest it should be late for the show.

PEKING—V

Dinner at the Grand Hotel, Peking, ended in a resolve to drive in rickshas to the Temple of Agriculture by moonlight. In four of us the feast had induced a mood that made such a resolve, at one o'clock in the morning, seem perfectly natural. But not prosaic. No passage through Peking in dancing rickshas down the soft dusty roads, in the filigree shadow of the carvings above the shop-fronts, in the soft light of paper lanterns, in the sound of cymbals and flutes from the theatres, could ever be prosaic.

In the moon-patched temple garden the illusion of tremulous ecstatic possibilities still held. By moonlight surely the old emperors would walk again to the sound of drums down the white shallow steps of the temple, to turn again the first furrow of the Imperial year with a plough drawn by dragons....

"Good Lord," said Robin. "S'quite spooky...."

And after a moment he said, "You'd almost think there was a light in that temple...." After another moment, "By George, there *is* a light in that temple."

"It's the moon ... surely."

But the moon, to-night, had a voice, a thin waving silver voice. Was it the voice of the dead herald of an awakening dead emperor? There was a yellow growing light in the temple. Were there banners moving in the light?

"Ou I say ... I'm damned if something beastly isn't going to appear. Let's get a move on."

The voice followed our rather tense retreat across the splintered puzzling shadows of the garden. "You'd almost think it was *your* name, Robin, that the voice was calling ..."

"Robin ... Robin ... Robin ..." It seemed a little starved, crazy, wandering Jew of a voice, trailing between stars. There was no sense to it. Let the damned old emperor put his hand to his plough again if he must and leave our Robin alone. Robin's white fixed face was turned over his shoulder towards where the imperial glow pulsed and expanded behind the screens and the pillars. Champagne, he thought, had never played him such a trick before.

"Robin ... Robin ... Robin ..." No human tongue could so spin out the syllables.

"Yes. It *is* calling me...." His incredulous, enchanted feet led us back towards the temple steps.

The glow in the temple grew and grew—and burst into reality. Emperors ... dragons ... banners ... shades of forgotten ceremonies of springtime....

"Hullo, *there* you are," said the friend with the lantern, "I was just looking for you.... I thought I heard you say something about coming here...."

OLD ARMIES AND OLD EMPERORS

The last war in north China being over and the next war not having begun, the gates of Peking once more opened tentatively to the world. I took advantage of this interlude to go forth with two or three donkey-loads of friends and other essentials to see the Great Wall.

Even against the evidence of my own eyes I cannot believe that the Great Wall of China is built of solid ordinary stones laid one upon the other. Rather it seems moulded out of the stuff of which the mountains themselves were made long ago, when the world was plastic and empty of all save possibilities. Men never built so sinuous a thing as that wall, I think—so sinuous and so aspiring. It disdains valleys, always it seeks the highest and steepest edges, throwing itself into wild extravagant loops to avoid low or commonplace levels. No angle appals it. As we walked along the broad way that runs along the top of the wall from watch-tower to watch-tower, the steps often became so steep that we had to hold on with our hands to the tangle of morning glory and larkspur and campanula that now takes the place of the disconsolate armies that used to man the wall.

I always somehow take for granted that those weatherbeaten far-flung old armies were disconsolate. I think it is pretty safe to assume that the Y.M.B.A.—(Young Men's Buddhist Association)—was not then what its equivalent is now. I tried to look down with a long—forgotten soldier's eye at the far yellow-patched plain of Manchuria from one of the steepest angles of the wall, and it seemed as if my heart missed its foothold, so to speak, and reeled on the brink of a spinning fall—down into the little walled town that guards the pass hundreds of feet below. It was a shock of relief to look over the edge of the wall and see no precipice—only the friendly grass and the wild flowers and the sheep cropping the roots of the wall close beneath.

We walked a little way down the paved camel road from the wall. The road is more ancient than the wall itself and, though still the supercilious camels occasionally pad into Manchuria along its broad crooked stones, it is moribund as a highway now. The railway has killed it.

We patronised that same railway in spite of its crime. We boarded a pig-train and sat on its step with our feet dangling over China. Pigs are far more valuable than immortal souls in China, hence we travelled to Nankow much more quickly than does the daily express.

From Nankow we rode three hours on dancing donkeys, through sunset, dusk, and dark to the greatest Ming Emperor's tomb. By starlight we reached his tall and austere gateway and in a corner of his outer hall we supped by candlelight. He was a silent yet splendid host. On every side he shared with us the immense and sombre feast of which he had dreamed. By starlight we could not see the heads of the great pillars of the hall or the chequered and peacock-coloured ceiling; we could barely see the dragoned outline of the side-pavilions in the courtyard.

But in the sunrise light as I unrolled myself from my blanket, I could see through the carven marble balustrade, the dragons and sea-waves of roofs awakening and disentangling their lines from those of the old gnarled trees that stood about them in an orange light.

I wonder if the Greatest Emperor, when he imagined that tremendous sky-line and those deep glowing arches and those strange shrines, ever remembered how little and forlorn a thing would lie beneath that thunderous magnificence. Did it seem right to him that the pale and brittle bones of a man should be the seed of such a flower?

As we rode away along an avenue of tall stone monsters, the other tombs stood humbly round the valley, taking their cue from the tomb of the Greatest Emperor—or perhaps only the vainest.... Great and small alike, they sent after us, across the gold-red heads of the *kaoliang*, the shimmer of their rippling yellow roofs, the royal glance of a silenced yet unfading order across a world unfaithful to its allegiance.

THE YANG-TSE RIVER

For a week I breathed gold air. For a week my eyes were attuned to the light on a golden river with rose-red ripples, running more and more fiercely as the days went by. Literally I bathed in yellow, for the bath-taps of the ship, connected apparently direct with the Father of Rivers, produced daily nothing but an opaque mustard-coloured section of whirlpool into which I plunged optimistically and from which I emerged feeling that at least I had tried to do my duty as an Anglo-Saxon.

The Yang-tse, a monster of temperament, was enjoying that autumnal irritation from which many of us suffer as winter draws in sight. Even during the comparatively peaceful journey up that stout and plebeian section of the river from Hankow to Ichang, I could not look at and realise the speed and passion of the water without feeling a slight contraction at the roots of my hair. After we left Ichang and began thundering up the gorges I will not disguise the fact that my hair stood straight on end, quivering a little at the tips as we curtseyed in a whirlpool or bounced from precipice to precipice—only missing actual contact, as it seemed, by an inch or two.

The rapids are plaited streams of yellow foam; their voices are various but always angry. Among the rapids the whirlpools build their nests—round deep nests lined with dark golden glass and frilled with a pale cream-coloured lace of foam. To fill up the precious space between the rapids and the whirlpools, ominous convex flowers of golden water boil up to the surface.

Water, as we were all taught at our mothers' knees, finds its own level, but the Yang-tse does not. It is super-water and scorns levels. Its whirlpools are as deep as craters, its rapids dig out abrupt valleys and pile up high tablelands of water to compensate for the valleys. Often at the foot of the cliffs on either side there is a sudden drop, or step down, in the water, and then a river within a river, much lower than the rest, divided from us by a permanent wave, and travelling absurdly the wrong way. Sometimes the junks were able, with their transparent, broad-shouldered sails spread, to follow the course of this rebel stream against the direction of the main river. More often they were pulled by dozens—scores—of trackers.

The trackers, sometimes in bright blue, sometimes in nothing at all, were strung like gay beads across the breast of the cliff, strung on a long string, one end of which was slung to a junk's mast. We seldom approached them closely enough to realise their humanity against their enormous backgrounds, to hear them chanting, to see them straining, slipping, bent, with their heads as low as their knees. But we could see more clearly the downcoming junks, for they took the middle of the stream and followed the will of the water. They swerved and span and plunged their bows into the water, their high golden sterns kicking and heaving. And we could hear the chanting and the shouting of the rowers and see the orchestral gestures of the leader, who danced and cursed amidships, directing their rowing.

Nobody is master of these wild waters. As our captain often remarked—"It's all a matter of joss ..." Only the great yellow cliffs dare to contradict the river, and they often suffer for their daring. Through the clefts in the broken cliffs you can see perspectives of mountains, heather-red and patched with woods and precipices. One village, divided in two by circumstances, flattened itself on two ledges connected by a ladder—two niches in the immense bald surface of a cliff. Up one sheer cliff a trail of niches seemed as faint to us as the track of an insect on fine sand. Legend claims that an attacking army cut those niches under cover of secret night and appeared, in a formidable halo of incredibility, in the midst of the unsuspecting little enemy town on the brow of the cliff. Legends blew about the noisy air of the river. There was a temple like a painted and enamelled toy at the head of a long shady flight of stone steps askew—and the bells of that temple, it seemed, rang of themselves when there was a fire among its little huddled attendant villages. Another temple had a bowl which used to be filled with rice in answer to prayer—until a greedy devotee brought a great barrel to replace the bowl, and thus rebuffed and checked forever the kindly hospitality of God.

Every night men from our ship swam to shore with a rope which, helped by our searchlight, they made fast to rocks and stakes. The most beautiful night was spent at Wu-shan, the guardian town of the longest gorge. To one steep bank of the river clung the little templed town of Wu-shan, its lower houses on stilts ankle-deep in the swift water, its upper houses turning curved roofs upward to the sunset. A slender pagoda was outlined against the pale bronze mountains. Over a finger of the river a one-spanned bridge, humped like a caterpillar, sprang, and, from the summit of this bridge, a tiny square guardhouse looked down at its own reflection. Behind the other bank of the river the sun sank in gold and rose. And the carved black outlines of a horned temple, steeply built, leaned against that sky. There was a tangle of old trees cut out of the near edge of the sky and a guardian griffin threw out its proud chest in the direction of Wu-shan across the river.

There was war in Szechuan—if you could call it war, for there were no posters about war. No pictures of strapping heroes encouraged those who felt neither strapping nor heroic to find out what tonic war could do for them. In Szechuan war advertised itself; one saw the war and one saw the heroes—which was unfortunate from the point of view of those who deal in war. Even the losers advertised the war. I watched the dead losers go, in procession but not in triumph, face downward down the river, threading their forlorn way through the plaited rapids, pausing indifferently in the quiet reaches where the water enfolded them like gold silk. I saw the less fortunate losers come to seek the protection of the mountains, the wounded slung painfully on poles carried by unfriendly coolies forced into service, or riding on bleeding and dying ponies. The unwounded also carried significant news of the glory of war; their sunken eyes saw nothing, their faces were like crumpled paper, they wavered on their feet. Only those of the vanquished who escaped first were strong enough to revenge themselves upon a cruel world. Like locusts they paused in their passing, and where they paused desolation entered.

When I first saw the steep villages opposite Chungking, they stood in calmness and isolation among their rice-fields. The blue smoke oozed domestically through the old thatch of the huts; under the eaves of the little shrines the joss-sticks bowed down among their ashes before the small golden faces of the gods; the clamour of the children in irresponsible village schools was mixed with the plaintive drums of the temples; the flooded rice-fields in scimitar and serpent shapes were dyked one above the other up the slopes at the feet of the mountains, and, across and across those narrow fields, like slow barges, the drooping buffaloes pulled ploughs through the water. The ploughmen sang;

only their sunburned upper halves showed above the water and those upper halves were made the more grotesque by hats as big as cartwheels.

When I saw those villages last, they were haunted; they were very silent; the children and the bells were not heard. No longer did the buffaloes work for their singing masters in the fields; their masters were themselves now slaves and beasts of burden. All countrymen—even the old men and the little boys—who had not been quick enough in finding places of concealment were caught and driven away before the bayonets of the army—itself a driven and hunted thing. I saw the peaceful men of those villages standing with blank dead faces, roped one to the other in long strings, waiting for their burdens. I saw them with backs bent under great loads, staggering before their captors, beaten or prodded with bayonets when they faltered or fell. I saw one man-hunt that seemed to me like a nightmare. Across the river the victors were coming into Chungking; the firing was incessant; we could see a little fluttering blue cloud of townspeople running ineffectually up and down at the foot of the city wall; every boat that dared to cross the river was surrounded by little abrupt fountains where the shots struck the water. High above our heads stray shots mewed and whined. Up the steep bank on our side of the river the last fugitives of the defeated army were slowly making their way; they seemed hardly conscious of being in danger, they were beyond panic, they went in little reeling groups and said no word, they were too weak to hurry. And I watched one who turned back toward the river; he could not carry even what remained to him of his possessions; he must seek a slave. Some river boatmen, leaning from the sterns of junks moored to the shore, were arresting the flight of the dead soldiers floating downstream, and taking from them boots and capes. Towards these coolies the exhausted soldier walked in uncertain curves; his chin was on his breast. Without seeming to look at the boatmen he made his way towards them. Without seeming to look at him, the boatmen herded nervously together and retreated to a further junk—and a further and a still further as he followed. There was silence among them and no hurry. Any one of the boatmen could have knocked the soldier down; he seemed to hold his rifle quite without purpose. On the furthest junk, the soldier, still, as it seemed, without raising his eyes, chose a man and drove him off. As far as I could see or hear there was no threat and no protest.

With the irritating detachment of Europeans in China I went to buy a pen in Chungking while the victorious army was at the city gates. Most of the shops were shuttered; most of the townspeople stood listening like frightened rabbits at the doors of their bolt-holes. One shop let us in to review its stock of pens, and while we were there a most strange and stormy sound of running bare feet came up the listening street, and a crowd of terrified citizens ran by, making no sound except the soft whispering sound of their running. The proprietor of the booth in which we were ran a barrier across his door and disappeared. We sat down unobtrusively in front of the little altar at the back of the booth. It seemed as if the street outside had fallen dead after that rush; the little bannered, crooked, tunnelled houses compressed their lips and stared blankly.

Finally two small soldiers of the advancing army came up the street with their bayonets pointing them on. Their faces were fixed in gross apoplectic appalled expressions; they did not look to either side.

When they had passed, the street, after some moments, relaxed. We made our way to the river gate. It was shut but, by mingling with some opportune retreating cavalry, we found our way out. We sat on the mud shore among the neutral crowds of beggars. I remember I had a bag of sweets and, on offering some to a little naked beggar boy, was nearly smothered in a charge of applicants for more. With other fugitive civilian citizens we rather disconsolately reviewed the probabilities of getting across the river before the fighting should begin. Every junk, every sampan, almost every plank, was commandeered by escaping soldiers. All the boatmen were hidden. We fawned upon the powers of darkness; we tried to step unobtrusively into the soldiers' sampans as they left the shore; we talked richly of money. Not money but a chance of life was the only currency in Chungking just then. Wherever we went the groups of Chinese civilians watched and followed, hoping that wherever British arrogance might lead the way, they might follow to safety. But they were disappointed. We were rather ignominiously rescued by an Englishman in a motor boat. And as I looked back at the less fortunate refugees left without friends upon that filthy shore, I was sorry to look so insolently safe.

The firing began then and, I think, by the time the moon came up, there were no losers left in Chungking to regret their loss. From the mountains some of them looked down at the flames dancing about the city of their failure; the others went face downward down the river and never looked up, or lay where they had fallen about the city gates, relieved at last of the horror of being hunted through those blind and twisted streets.

The war in Chungking provided cover for the smuggling of opium on board our departing ship. Almost every Chinese passenger and sailor had a hand in this. The chief officer spent the first day of the return journey in sniffing his way from cache to cache. He was a keennosed man and by evening his cabin was overflowing with confiscated opium in every form.

When we tied up that evening, half-a-dozen Chinese soldiers came on board to welcome us and at the same time to say that any opium we had on board would be in turn welcome to their officers. Our captain, with Western terseness, took out his watch and gave his visitors one minute to disappear in. At the end of the minute, he explained, he proposed to blow the alarm syren for a crew from a neighbouring British gunboat. The poor soldiers spent their minute uncomfortably in wondering whether a beating at the hands of English sailors was preferable to a beating at the hands of their own opium-hungry officers. At the end of the minute the syren squawked, and one of the soldiers, feeling that something must be done to preserve the dignity of Chinese arms, stepped forward and, with a neat, snake-like gesture, stabbed the chief engineer. The engineer did not at once realise what had happened to him; he was stabbed through the muscles under his arm. He was able to join in a shout of warning to us. For there we were, an exasperating, superior British audience, standing in a bovine ring round the scene of the poor soldiers' dilemma. The soldiers, noticing their public situation, became more and more annoyed with the British and all their ways; they climbed quickly back into their boat and, with another dramatic gesture, turned their revolvers upon us—upon *us*—a little gentle herd of inquisitive globe-trotters, armed only with cameras, field-glasses and Mosquitol.

I never in my life saw such a sudden and complete slump in Anglo-Saxon superiority. Personally, I jumped about thirty feet to the other side of the deck-house. The deck became a tangle of respectable British citizens, dignified but one short second before, now intertwined with Chinese stewards behind the flimsy canvas deck-chairs. But no shot was fired. The searchlight, that most rude and disconcerting weapon, turned its eye upon the enemy. The squawk of the gunboat's syren was heard above the roar of the river. The soldiers, standing in their released boat and with their revolvers still pointing, as it seemed,

54

at my fifth rib, were snatched away by the eager river. They dwindled like an unnatural dream in the unwinking glare of the searchlight.

INDIA—I

THE DIVERTED ATTENTION

This is the thing that I remember best about Ceylon. Along the road beside the sea to the Galle Face Hotel, little naked boys lie in wait for the rickshas. They keep pace with you, their little fat feet fly like windmills and beat the ground two or three times to every stride of the ricksha man. When they grow up they will be ricksha men too, but at present they make that noble calling a little ridiculous. The ricksha man rebukes them, but they cannot be snubbed; they must do their stunts before they admit defeat. "Is a lung way to Tippererry ... goodbay Luster Squah." Wonderful to be able to carry such a true little thin voice on such twinkling frantic legs! Yellow flowers are thrown in your lap to show that the stunt is over. Shortness of leg will tell in the end. They fall back and the ricksha springs forward in renewed dignity.

I have always suffered from diverted attention. Of the two distinct general compartments of my mind, the one into which the sun most rarely shines is the one reserved for soul-stirring impressions. The other compartment, filled with little curious happenings connected with everything or nothing, with spiders and spaghetti, boarding-house keepers and beetles, puppies and Prime Ministers, is constantly in use, with the blinds always drawn up.

While it is possible, I am told, to absorb the Taj Mahal, hold it for a time in the heart and then give it back to the world as a sonata or a sonnet, delight can be found at the same time in the beetles and the lizards and the tourists that wriggle in and out of its crannies. I suppose that noble people, on seeing the Taj, concentrate entirely on the sonnet department and walk about on the lizards and the beetles and the tourists without noticing them. Yet, in my case, I must confess that if a monkey and a minaret were competing for my attention, the monkey would almost certainly win.

My memory of Akbar's tomb at Sikanderabad is thrown out of perspective by the intrusion of a tree in the garden which was quivering with the presence of a great many peculiarly charming gibbons. They had grey velvet coats and black earnest faces. One realised suddenly that there were hundreds of live gibbons to one dead Akbar. From every loophole in their great green fortress, their kindly perplexed faces looked out between grey hands parting the leaves of the tree.

I do not think I shall lightly forget the Taj Mahal. It stands on the horizon of my memory like a tall cloud with an opal glow on it. Still, I cannot forget the expressions of the gharry horses waiting outside for the tourists. There is something about gharry horses that reminds me of the agonies of sympathy I went through as a child at the village races, when I saw the milkman's little fat worthy pony lined up for the start side by side with the squire's thoroughbred exquisites. "Not a chance, not a chance—yet it's preening itself, it's imagining how it will look with the blue cockade of honour behind its ear. 'After all,' it's thinking, 'stranger things have happened....'" And still, now that I am grown-up, when I drive through the streets of Calcutta listening to talk about the pacification of Islam, and now and then making a keenly intelligent comment like, "Great Scot, but that was Mr. Lloyd George's fault, wasn't it?...", all the time I am looking at the faces of the gharry horses. They are vulgar, necessary little horses and nobody fastidious admires them. But they wear blue bead necklaces just behind their ears and they trot with an industrious and wistfully hopeful look as if they were saying, "Well, what price these darn thoroughbreds and Rolls Royces now? I've got my beads on...." And they smile at one another—rather a forced, tentatively boasting smile—when a buffalo goes by. "Poor old slowcoach ... no beads for him...."

Of course there are also the sad members of the beef family to be sorry for, but there is seldom much life or vanity in their eyes. Bulls, of course, are different. Holy bulls were the heroes of my visit to Benares. They stand at Benares street corners, horn to horn, eating sacred marigolds which they have no intention of paying for, and cynically discussing the passing pilgrims and globe-trotters. They come and go at no man's orders; they are the tigers of that jungle of temples. Holiness crowns them—yet you can see they think nothing of holiness. They wear expedient holiness for the comfort of it, as the medieval popes used to wear it. On the steep crowded bank of the Ganges, priests dance and howl and gash themselves and lie on beds of spikes and mix their hair with mud—and the imperious smooth bulls watch them passionlessly, saying one to another, "There—that's what comes of taking things too seriously ..." On the opposite bank of the Ganges there is nothing and nobody, because of the legend that anyone chancing to die on that side is born again as an ass or a woman. But the bulls probably warn one another that any bull who dies in Benares risks being born again as a man. For they alone in Benares do not follow and cry after death. At the edge of the river the pilgrims bathe; they dip and they cry out and dip again; the holy glitter of the river wraps them away from everything but prayer—prayer that some day death in this holy place may crown their pinnacle of holiness. Sometimes they are so importunate that they succeed; among the thousands of pilgrims, of whom so many are old, there are always some who find dear death on the edge of the brown blessed water. And these, after a lying-in-state on pyres among flames on a ledge of the river bank, are given to the river itself to carry away and seal with holiness.

But death is not the river's only blessing. A bull and I leaned on a wall and watched a marriage in the water. A man and a woman knotted their robes together and dipped down side by side, and, as they dipped, a little boy priest threw marigolds over them. "Waste of good marigolds ..." grumbled the bull. I pointed out something that I knew would annoy him more—a cow, in the distance, being reverently bathed in the holy river by a peasant and his wife. The bull tossed his horns. "Good Lord," he snorted, "a cow—a female *cow*—what are we coming to? I thought India was sound on the feminist question at least...."

Cows in India occupy the same position in society as women did in England before they got the vote. Woman was revered but not encouraged. Her life was one long obstacle-race owing to the anxiety of man to put pedestals at her feet. While she was falling over the pedestals she was soothingly told, that she must occupy a Place Apart—and indeed, so far Apart did her Place prove to be, that it was practically out of earshot. The cow in India finds her position equally lofty and tiresome. You practically never see a happy cow in India. Nobody east of Suez, of course, ever dares to say anything even remotely carnivorous to a cow, yet there is something in her luminously myopic eye, and in her cheek grooved by a perpetual tear, that suggests that her life is empty of delight. She must know that she holds half India's politics in the hollow of her hoof; like our mothers, she must have been constantly told how incalculable is her indirect influence on her country's destiny—yet she is humiliated and unsatisfied.

And oxen.... Seeing them crawling moodily along, buried from stem to stern under an outrageous superstructure of dry goods, the weight of which seems to bear more heavily on their necks than on the waggon wheels, one cannot think that they derive any real gratification from the knowledge that no orthodox Hindu would eat them. It can give them no more than a passing and superficial pleasure to feel that their masters revere them enough to carve elaborate freehand curves in their hides. The ox must often reflect bitterly on the fact that the gods, after starting well by setting his family on a pedestal of sacred tradition, should have spoilt the whole thing by giving him a hump. That hump is the undoing of the Indian branch of the beef family. Nobody could possibly see that hump without wishing to fit a yoke in front of it. No other physical feature has ever been so obviously designed for the use of industrious man as is the hump. Divorce the hump from the yoke and where is the use of it? The crows, to be sure, are in the habit of using it as a vantage point on which to stand while surveying the rest of the animal in search of ticks—but this can hardly be said to constitute a *raison d'être* for the hump. No, if you wear a hump you have to crown it with a yoke, and if you wear a yoke and have a heartless jodelling master sitting on it all day, pulling at a string that is threaded through your nose and beating you on a sore place on your buttock, where is the fun of belonging to a reverend family? You might just as well be a common lay buffalo.

Yet, with all this, anyone can see that the buffalo is a long way behind the ox in the social scale. There is no compensation for being born a buffalo; he has no lofty traditions at all—and he knows it. The only legend in his family connects him bluntly with Sin. You may often see rude caricatures of his homely and unlucky figure ramping in and out of Hindu pictures in company with headless bodies and bodiless heads and demons and women and other attributes of hell. Even this doubtful sport is, one fears, purely legendary; no decent self-respecting demon would ever condescend to ramp with a buffalo. The buffalo knows that; he knows everything about himself; he has no illusions—you can read that in his eyes. The yoke wedged under his horns prevents him from looking round to see what a poor figure his partner is cutting, but he needs no reminder—he knows. He knows that he and his partner and his mother and all his family are the plainest and least dainty creatures on the face of the earth—with the possible exception of the wart-hog. Even when he was a calf, his mother used to contemplate him dubiously. Many people have loved cows, and even poets have mentioned them, but nobody has ever loved a buffalo. You could not love or respect a creature which, during the whole course of evolution, has never decided whether to be a bald or a hairy beast. After earnest study of the faces of the buffaloes on Chowringhee, I cannot even say that they have beautiful souls. Of almost anyone hopelessly plain, it is fairly safe to say—"Yes, not exactly *pretty*—but *how* good-hearted...." Not so of the unfortunate buffalo. No heart or soul shines out of his eyes at all; they are matt eyes, anguished, but not poetically so. Sometimes buffaloes are seen sitting like desert islands in ponds, or, better still, in running streams with miniature breakers surging against their bleak headlands. At such times a faint smear of tranquillity, so to speak, may be seen by the keen observer on the horny surface of the buffalo's eye and in the twitch of his sad unstarched ear, but there is nothing at all radiant about the *tout ensemble*. Sometimes the water is so deep that only a mud-coated nose and a few eyelashes are seen above the surface. In this pose the buffalo is seen to best advantage, but, even so, no-one but a crocodile would bother to look twice at him.

The buffalo's only attempt at vanity or individuality is expressed in the cut and angle of his horns. Most buffaloes wear their horns with pessimism and without chic. But some try feebly to imitate the brisker angle affected by their neighbours, the oxen. I once saw a buffalo with one horn up and one down; the effect was original and almost waggish. I saw another whose horns made an almost perfect circle above his yoke, and the tips overlapped. If that buffalo had been mine I would have tied the tips together with a pale blue hair-ribbon. And then all the other buffaloes on Chowringhee would have seen it and smiled at last, saying, "There goes the one member of our race whom somebody loves."

A buffalo fainted at my feet once. I heard a noise like a train gathering steam, and realised that it was the stertorous breathing of a fainting buffalo. Its attendant was beating it, but it was past minding that. I went into the Army and Navy Stores and asked what facilities they had for reviving fainting buffaloes. The military gentleman at the door said "None." He seemed a little ruffled. Nevertheless, after some argument, I re-emerged at the head of a file of coolies carrying the Society's fire-buckets. These we emptied on to the buffalo and forced a few drops into its drooping mouth. It revived immediately and proceeded on its way, saying to itself, "No, nobody loves me ... even when I faint I am made a fool of on the public streets by stray female novelists...."

All social functions are distorted for me by my eye for the domestic lizard. Every room in Calcutta has its lizard, a pale, languid, fawn-coloured creature with a throbbing throat, who meditates on vertical or upside-down surfaces, and occasionally expresses his conclusions in a very loud unexpected voice. The lizards eat the insects in the rooms, but the one in my bedroom is rather a slacker. He refuses to tackle an enormous spider, like an animated eight-legged horse-chestnut, which has insolently made its home on my lizard's beat. I do not know how the lizards of a house apportion the various rooms, but I think that drawing-room lizards are selected for the loudness of their voices. Often at a party, when I think I have been listening to my hostess complaining of high prices, I find myself replying to a remark by the lizard. A sporting lizard with a good figure and a well-wielded accurate tongue can hold my attention against any human rivalry. And even when my mind wanders from that it is only in order to devote itself to the thin didactic wailing of the kites above the roof, or the hoarse cursings and dry-cleaning operations of the grey-hooded crows outside the window, or the hysteria of the brain-fever bird—"So there, so *there*, so THERE...." When I was trying to be affable at a garden-party once, a kite swooped down and removed a rather valued sandwich from my plate, knocking my hat awry as it did so. Evidently even the kites know how much undue attention I pay to the world that is really theirs rather than mine. So they have no reverence for me.

I went on a Christmas visit to eleven elephants in Rajputana. I had never met an elephant as man to man—or elephant to elephant—before, except, of course, in the Zoo, where they are rather consciously exotic. But there in the jungle in Rajputana, nothing was allowed to be exotic—not even the jewelled Maharajah, into the radius of whose immense hospitality I was accidentally swept. Our gorgeous camp, which had a hint of old leisurely pretty battlefields about it, the glittering turbaned soldier at the door of each frilled and painted tent, the huge tall waggonette drawn by two trotting camels, the cramped, mazy, romantic ways of the castle, the little yellow capital city of the kingdom ... none of these were exotic, boxed in, as they were, by that clear burning sky and that infinite round horizon. Large bald-faced wistful monkeys stood out conspicuously against the low yellow wilderness that—in Rajputana—is called the jungle; blackbuck and nil-ghai frequented the near horizon unashamed; jackals sat as publicly as dogs in the shade of shrivelled shrubs, and as for the peacocks and the kingfishers and the hoopoes, they took upon themselves the duty of flowers in that sad unbounded garden.

So that when, for the first time, I motored to a meet with the intention of watching falcons and a tame lynx bring hares or tigers—(and what not)—to my feet, it did not seem fantastic to find myself surrounded by a high wall of benevolent elephant faces. I don't know anybody else with such a humorous face as an elephant; each of its little eyes is set in a wreath of smiles, and when it lies down to let you mount—forelegs straight out forward, back legs straight out backward—it is a sort of idealised Fatty Arbuckle.

I chose my mount for the hunt, a small merry elephant with a kind of antimacassar painted in scarlet on its brow. I climbed on to its obligingly recumbent form by means of a ladder and sat on a canvas pad, holding on desperately to the waist-belt of a liveried minion who sat astride of the elephant's neck wielding a bi-dent—(if there is no such word as bi-dent—why not?). My elephant had a playful way of trumpeting through a madly agitated trunk when it was either bored or excited. The sound was rather like changing gears on a Ford car, and the result was that passers-by were soaked to the skin.

The field consisted of about forty guests, some mounted on horses, some on ponies and some on elephants. The elephant contingent was sub-divided into olders and wisers, sitting in furnished pavilions on tall slow elephants of the super-dreadnought type, and youngers and silliers like me, who took the destroyers' part in the fleet, rattling up and down on the saddles of little rampageous elephants-made-for-two. There was also the Maharajah, carrying a handsome eagle-like bird on his wrist, and a large number of minions, carrying hooded hawks, and an ox-cart, carrying an irascible-looking blindfolded lynx. The ox-cart hurried industriously after the hunt, but always arrived too late, to the increasing annoyance of the lynx.

Whenever the hawks were released, the whole field cheered loudly. Perhaps this well-meant encouragement disconcerted the hawks, for, although the ground was knee-deep in game—hares, partridges and deer splashing on all sides from under our charging feet—the birds either glued themselves to the sky, or else flew straight to the highest tree in sight and sat on it, moodily putting their feathers in order. Nearly all our time was spent in luring sulky hawks from trees by means of false decoy-birds flapped about the ground with string. The elephants were much more keen, running heavily after every hare they saw and trying to soar after the soaring partridges. My elephant nervously uprooted and stuffed into its mouth young shrubs as it thundered along, trumpeting breathlessly between mouthfuls. I was sorry that no hare was sporting enough to allow itself to be caught by these means.

Trying to forget its empty bag, my elephant led the stately procession home at sunset through the little yellow sandy town that is the capital of our Maharajah's kingdom. In the torchlit booths the citizens bowed and blessed the procession in slow sing-song. The proud prudish faces of the camels seemed to boast of their gaudy burdens as they passed us; little dusty children, naked except for silver anklets, asked for alms in high metallic voices and, outside a temple, two fierce urgent bells rang one against the other.

I watched the elephants in lighter vein next day running a race. Their riders were mostly nervous amateurs, who knew no word of elephant language and saw no difference between *Hut* and *Hell*. (If this should meet the eye of an elephant, I hope he will excuse my spelling, which is purely phonetic.) The elephants smiled in a long row but, smile they never so wisely, they entirely failed to grasp the theory of the entertainment. They thought that they were taking part in a kind of royal musical ride, and when, at the sound of the pistol shot, they moved forward with serene dignity, not even the babel of shrieks and curses from the amateurs on their backs could induce them to fall out of line. In a perfect row they started; in a perfect row they proceeded very slowly along the track, pensively waving their trunks to keep one another in step; in a perfect row they breasted the tape at the other end. And then they all sighed happily, satisfied to feel that they had done their duty. It was the most impressive race I ever saw.

INDIA—II

Bengal's Legislative Council was re-born almost under my eye; her Ship of State, for the first time manned by Indians, was launched by the Duke of Connaught in February 1921. Among other Calcutta women I had permission to witness this historic ceremony. Nevertheless, though I and the other women put on our most ceremonious hats or *saris* and flourished grass-green passes, the authorities decreed, on second thoughts, that the occasion was too historic for the eye of woman.

Women come to India, I understand, either because they are married to empire builders or because they want to be. They are expected to learn to play bridge well, to dance well in the manner of about two years ago, and to know what to wear at the races. To take an interest in India is, on the other hand, most unladylike. A nice woman may go so far as to say sometimes, "My dear, I'm *simply terrified* of these fiendish revolutionaries and things, I sometimes think they'd like to blow us all up in our beds." A kind of imperial district visiting is also permitted and one may hear a Perfect Lady talk about "My little Thursday Ranees", to whom she teaches leather-work or basket-making. But to find a woman going farther than this, or to hear her admit that she has come to India to see India, will make any well-brought-up empire builder blush. The younger he is, the pinker he blushes.

India is the only country I ever visited where the young are truly Victorian. Young people in India still talk of chaperones and minxes and not-quite-of-our-class-my-dear. They share with their seniors their confusion and dislike at the mention of Epstein and Women-in-Men's-Professions and Bernard Shaw and sitting on the floor and the Labour Party. There are no youngers and silliers in India to worry the olders and wisers. Everyone is modelled on Kipling. The only adventure left is a flirtation with someone else's husband or wife, and these flirtations seem always to be quotations from Kipling—deliciously shocking. Perfect Ladies are everywhere found being shocked at other Perfect Ladies on grounds that would make King's Road, Chelsea, smile.

Nearly everyone in India simply *adores* reading or drawing or music or poker-work or just Art. But the men are too busy Keeping Fit in the intervals of empire-building to indulge themselves in their delight. And the women—"Of course, my dear, there's *nothing* I should like better, but I have a houseful of servants and a kiddie to look after and then one simply *has* to go to the club in the afternoon—I tell you I never have a *second*."

And this from men and women whose youth has found them at a time when youth is at last allowed to go unchained—and found them, too, in one of the most fantastic countries in the world.

Women were therefore allowed, on the occasion of the opening of Bengal's first Indian Legislative Council, to sit and look as charming as possible on the stairs, to see the pretty uniforms, to curtsey to the Duke as he arrived and to listen to a far-off bee-like sound which was the noise of the Ship of State being launched.

The launching of a ship is usually marked by the breaking of a bottle of wine, but over Bengal's ship they broke casks of honey. Everyone spoke affabilities, the atmosphere was sticky with sugar—even we banished women could grasp that. Where do the optimists go when their speeches are done? Hopers only seem to hope in public.

It goes without saying—except in the papers, where nothing goes without saying—that the Duke of Connaught opened the Council in a way that justified the loud applause that reached us even in our exile. But I was haunted all the time by the possibilities of an impossible dream—of another kind of opening of a democratic council. What if this Indian Parliament—representing, it is said, the voice of India— had been opened by the voiceless Indian? What if a little thin dust-coloured peasant, chosen on the Unknown Soldier principle, had stood in that hall—the hall being empty of pretty soldiers? He would have thrown out his arms (I dreamed), and cried, "This is my voice.... At last I have found my voice...."

It was, of course, a silly dream, for the affair would not have been half so pretty without the uniforms. And there would have been no occasion for the Perfect Ladies to wear their best hats. I remembered putting on my best hat a week or two before in order to go and see Mahatma Gandhi. It was lost on him—in fact I found that he had only

65

accorded me the interview under the impression that I was a man. He treated me as a saint might treat an uninstructed cherub. He was very gentle and tired-looking; his nearly white hair was cropped on a high narrow head. His chin was bowed upon his breast and he looked upward at me out of sunken eyes over a ridge of brow. He talked to me in extremely accurate, forensic, English and did not at all want to hear my comments. If he, in his white homespun, looking with eyes that did not see politeness, had opened that council, I think our sweet words would have fallen on dumbness and our pretty hats and uniforms and French dresses would have dissolved in sombre Indian dust.

A few days later, wisely disguising myself, not this time as a Lady, but as the Press, I found my way into the council hall again. This time I had a commanding view of a waving field of turbans and fezes, diversified by some examples of the British national head-dress—the bald spot on the top.

Sir Shamsul Huda, the President, the Portia-like effect of whose clothes was rather contradicted by his fine grey beard, was obviously suffering from the natural doubt of the debutant. In this feeling he was evidently not alone for, from beginning to end, the proceedings were like a game of which nobody knows the rules. One or two Englishmen had evidently been poring over the *Encyclopædia* at the Parliamentary Procedure page, and helpfully fluttered from minister to minister, from member to member, explaining sometimes what should be done but more often what should not be done—generally after someone had begun to do it. Whenever a member asked a question, a minister rose to explain why that question did not arise, on which all the members' faces fell. There was a natural desire to debate matters which did not lie within the province of the Council but had already been settled by the Government of India. The Council was verbally feeling its way round its boundaries, and much precious tongue-power was wasted on the process.

The first division in the life of the Council was taken on a question of salary and was a great success as a diversion. One or two members actually skipped with suppressed giggles into the lobby.

To me, one of the most noticeable things was the immediate division between youth and age. It is, apparently, a fact that all parliaments automatically take this formation, even on the first day of their lives. And in all parliaments the old men always *seem* to have the power on their side. Perhaps this *seeming* is their compensation.

INDIA—III

I never got a job in India—unless lying in bed in hospital, writing desperately sprightly articles for newspapers, can be called a job. But I was very well-befriended, and was able, at times, to give a rather feeble imitation of a Globe-trotter in India. The nine Delhis have almost all been looked at by me. In Delhi and in Agra I have stood in the flowery starry net of light that lies on the air inside the filigree marble screens and windows—those thin lace veils of interthreaded stone. I have pitied the poor hermit of Fatehpur-Sikri who, for a successful stroke of magic wrought upon a queen, was gratefully punished by having his darling lonely hill encrusted and pinnacled with a king's city, and his body, which must have loved to lie upon grass and flowers, buried at last in a marble and mother-o'-pearl shrine. I was introduced to another miracle—Monsieur Clémenceau, as he arrived at a station after a tiger shoot. He looked old and cold but proud. "I have shot two tigers," he said, wrapping himself jerkily in a big shawl. The Indian who was his host said, "I have shot a hundred and five." "But ... when one is eighty ... two tigers ..." said the old Tiger, looking for a moment, in spite of his little smile, snubbed like a child. He cried out for his manservant as though he were calling his Nannie, and wanted many things done immediately, all at once. "One of the tigers he shot," said the Indian, "was already——" But we did not want to hear, and the old man pulled his shawl up round his ears.

I made a little wandering slow journey through Eastern Bengal to the edge of Assam with Cornelia Sorabji, who is nearly a fairy but cannot be a Perfect Lady, I suppose, since she commits the unladylike mistake of working for and loving India. On the Brahmapootra river the crescent fishing-boats lay like new moons on the water, and between them and the sand-dunes the dwelling boats floated, square and matronly, with a prosaic noise of clucking hens and whooping babies, under square-shouldered sails drawn together at the foot like great honey-coloured fans. The little plaited houses on the shore had humped roofs like the backs of whippets, and the mango trees, blossoming, always seemed to have the sun on them, even at twilight or at dawn. I remember the velvety stammering music of a flute played by one of the Indian peasant travellers to an accompaniment of lapping river-ripples and the distant voices of hauling fishermen.

I took another river-journey. The Sunderbunds look like a bath sponge on the map, between Calcutta and the sea. Clans of primitive Indians, who have scarcely heard of, and almost certainly do not appreciate, the blessings of British rule, live among those steamy ravelled waterways. Tigers do very well too; the tigers of the Sunderbunds have brought the name of Bengal to the fore in the tiger world. Yet I do not know how man or tiger can grow to normal size in those jungles. The low brush is everywhere so knotted and knitted together that, one would imagine, nothing larger than a mouse could penetrate it. I daresay, however, that there are tunnelled runs through the jungle, invisible to travellers on the waterways—probably fat, low, bold runs for the tigers, carefully avoided by the tall clever runs of men, and—apart from either of these two—very slender, cautious, haunted runs for the deer and defenceless delicate things.

Monkeys, at any rate, need only the air and a few swinging upper twigs for their travelling. There were Frenchmen on board our little ship who fired at the monkeys. They fired at everything they saw but, fortunately, they scarcely ever hit anything. The monkeys, fired on, lost their heads like children, screamed, threw up their little hands, sprang wildly about. A solid mass of public opinion on our boat decided against any more firing on monkeys. Yet no-one except me was sorry for the crocodiles. The crocodiles lay asleep on the grey mud banks. Little buttonhook smiles of peace and complacency curled the corners of their mouths. But our Frenchmen fired at them. A crocodile, I am told, cannot be killed except by a shot through a special soft bit of skin at the throat. But I daresay even Achilles could be worried by a mosquito on any part of his invulnerable body, and certainly a crocodile can be very much shocked—in its sensibilities at least—by a rattle of shots against any part of its carefully armoured figure. Most painful to me was the sight of the rude awakening, the dreadful change from tranquillity to fury on the mobile features of the hit crocodile. It started to attention, coughed out a terrible oath, opened its mouth—which was, if I may so express it, curiously full of *mouth*, as thickly cushioned as an arm-chair and only unobtrusively frilled with teeth—and, with fish-like agility, whipped itself quickly into the water. Its first intention obviously was to attack us and revenge itself. But after a few seconds the size of our steamboat made an impression and the crocodile, after flouncing and splashing about in disgust, submerged to sulk.

There was, as far as I was concerned, one tiger in the Sunderbunds—and indeed it is still there, as far as I know, for no shot from our boat touched it. I had great difficulty in seeing the creature at all. On the cry of "Tiger, tiger...." I looked smartly about for something burning bright in the forests of the night. I thought I should see a splash as blatant as a sunflower against the grey thicket and grey mud. There was nothing. I was within a wink of seeing absolutely nothing at all. All I can swear to was a hinted cringing shape as low—it seemed—as a dachshund and in a much duller shade of brown. It moved into a dim place, stood for a few seconds and then, when the firing began, dissolved like butter in a pan.

After a few days we reached a village which is connected by an amphibious light railway with Calcutta. By train my friends were obliged to return, but I stayed behind, intending to take the next boat home and see more tigers. As soon as train and friends were gone, I directed Lars Porsena, my servant, to make enquiries. He discovered that there was no boat for three days, no train till next day and that there was either no dak-bungalow or else it was out of repair. There were no sahibs or mem-sahibs in the village, added Lars Porsena hopelessly. But I found one as I was walking disconsolately along the mud shore. He was an engineer and of course a Scot. He was talking to an Indian river-captain, who wore balloon trousers, a kind of fez and a very pretty little jade-green sleeveless jacket. They were at that moment setting off to navigate back to Calcutta a broken steamboat for repair. "She has no lichts," said the engineer. "There's no beds in herr cabins. She has a leest and I'm a wee thing doubtful but what she might turrn turrtle," but he kindly took on board a crateful of chickens for my consumption, and so we started. The whole plan depressed Lars Porsena. He did not like me to sleep on a table in a dismantled cabin. He did not like me to darn the engineer's socks by the light of a candle stuck in a bottle. He felt that British prestige suffered by the fact that hot water had to be brought to my cabin in an old Yellow Cling Peach can.

We lived on chicken that had barely ceased to breathe and on whiskies and sodas. If my appearance had not made the crate of chickens necessary, the engineer would, I suppose, have dispensed with that

69

half of the menu. A music-hall joke justified! We told each other the stories of our lives; we whistled all the tunes we knew to each other and he offended me by calling old ballad-tunes "heem-tunes". Every evening—since we had no lights—we tied up to the shore and hung our one lantern out. The cries and howls and roars and chatterings of the forest seemed very close. But we never saw a tiger. We saw glades lighted and shadowed with deer. They had delicate triangular heads like flowers on the thin upright stems of their necks. They watched us pass with an alert reproachful stare, but they never fled because we— fortunately—lacked guns.

One night we had to tie up within range of the stray waves of the sea. The crippled boat heaved with a sort of imbecile exaggeration. The Scot stood thoughtfully about, feeling her pulse, and remarking that we were not more than a few minutes' swim from land and that the crocodiles often missed their man. He was an excellent and careful nurse to the poor boat in his charge, and he triumphed at last, bringing the invalid safely into Calcutta.

Calcutta was like a steaming kettle, hissing with the voices of kites and frogs. An accurately levelled ceiling of white mist was suspended above the broad Maidan, slung between the white domed Memorial and the big business buildings. At the river's edge the cargo ships coughed and cursed and boasted but, for the moment, as I crossed the Maidan, I did not envy them. I was just home from my own little odd voyage and would not have exchanged it.

INDIA—IV

The Pundit and his second wife came to tea. The upper part of the Pundit's body was "foreign style" except for the very small neat turban that surmounted his large aggrieved brown face; his dark alpaca coat was a tribute to the truly British rite of five o'clock tea. But his legs were draped in loopings of spotless white cotton beside which the trousers of imperial Britain looked constrained and bourgeois.

The Pundit's second wife was nearly thirteen years old. She held the hand of her stepdaughter—her senior—very nervously, but this consolation was intermittent, for, whenever anyone spoke to her or looked at her, both her hands must be disengaged and clasped before her little thin nodding nose in an attitude of prayer. The plea—hurt *Don't hurt me*—shone through that little polite gesture and was her only reproach to society or comment on her lot. She wore a rich wine-coloured *sari* and, as she sat looking extremely small on the sofa beside her large English hostess, her little tinselled beaded feet trod nervously upon each other. She would not eat or drink; she only bobbed and prayed when dishes were offered to her.

The Pundit, who was perhaps thirty years older than she was, sat opposite, looking critically at his second wife. It was his intention, he said, that she should be a woman of the world, not a *pardah nashin*. He wished her worldliness to be achieved within the year, for he intended to take her to England almost at once and expected her to be able to entertain his friends and take her proper and assured place in the world. It was time, he said, that Indian women should help their husbands in the social duties that the Empire demanded of prominent men like himself. He intended to engage a competent lady secretary, an Englishwoman, to instruct his wife in the necessary worldliness. We all looked at the Pundit's wife and her hands sprang together and her quivering chin jerked down on her breast as she caught the look.

Our hostess rose and found in a drawer an Indian doll, looking rigidly and brazenly from beneath its gaudy *sari*.

The Pundit's second wife forgot to pray before taking the doll into her arms. "Ai ai," she said, arranging its robe, "Ai ai, ai ai."

She would have thought her own enthusiasm very coarse and vulgar if she had stopped to realise it. Perhaps the Pundit thought that she was not quite living up to her own important position, for he looked quickly away from her and said, "Dolls like these are often made by Indian families to accustom their young daughters to the meaning of marriage. First a male doll is given, then a female doll, and finally, one by one, young dolls. In this way innocence is instructed."

His second wife was feeling the doll's face with a finger like the tiny brown frond of a fern. "Ai ai ..." she was saying in a most secret voice. "Ai ai ai...."

THE STATES AGAIN—I

In England, after three years, I tied the knot of the rather humble ravelled thread of my journeying round the world.

I got married and spent six months of arduous leisure in a carefree re-visiting of that America I had once crossed with suspense and with much counting of pennies.

Ignorance is the impetus that pushes all travellers from their starting-points. We travel because we do not know. We know that we do not know the best before we start. That is why we start. But we forget that we do not know the worst either. That is why we come back. From the furious tourist who discovers too late that the daily delivery of the *Morning Post* is scarcely ever achieved in foreign lands, to the square-jawed traditional hero who finds himself alone without ammunition face to face with an exasperated tigress, we all find that, in making ourselves the guests of strange lands, we reckon without our hosts. We are more likely to imagine our sensations on first seeing the Taj Mahal than to anticipate the inconvenience caused by the eating of our trousseaux by white ants. It is, of course, a happy thing that we have optimistic imaginations to make fools—or, in other words, tourists—of us all. At least it is a happy thing for hotel-keepers, hungry tigresses, white ants and what not. But it is, I find, a doubtful honour to be more of a fool than any one else.

Nobody but a true fool tries to cross the United States in a Ford car in the middle of winter. Fools in a minor degree do it fairly often in summer, but the fools who cross in winter are the princes of their kind. We are converted to this doctrine now; yet, with our folly and forty-six hundred miles safely in our past, we are rather proud of being princes of our kind.

There are several highways across the North American continent, and this fact alone fools travellers. Highway is a word with an easy and comfortable sound to the ears of all but those who have already motored across the States. Actually the use of the word in this connection is an act of faith, and very beautiful. It means that some day Ford-errants, or their successors, will be able to run singing, without changing gears, on a road like a taut wire stretched from the sunrise to the sunset. Let us not dwell on the disappointing fact that, by that time, all the trans-continental fools will be inefficiently using aeroplanes, and the only improvement will be that they will fall into air-pockets instead of bog-holes, and so end their folly and their difficulties once and for all. At present, however, the winter highway is very inadequate as a way and can hardly be called high. The winter route must be the most southerly possible and, on the "Old Spanish Trail", the Continental Divide is only six thousand feet high. Mostly the trail burrows in swamps like a mud-turtle, ploughs its way humbly through deep unstable sands or explores the edges of dead inland seas and slow red rivers.

These are the states through which we passed: N.Y., N.J., Pa., Del., Md., D.C., Va., N.C., S.C., Ga., Ala., Miss., La., Tex., N.M., Ariz., and Calif. I hope this is perfectly clear.

Humility is the first thing expected of a Ford owner. It is the last thing the Ford owner feels. We have never before owned anything that ran on wheels but, now that we own a Ford called Stephanie, Pierce Arrows and Rolls Royces are nothing to us. Believe it or not—on a good road we could pass every known make of car except a Ford, and nothing but a Ford ever dared to pass us.

Stephanie is the newest model; her voice is like that of the nightjar in midsummer; her profile is Grecian in its exquisite simplicity. She hails from Connecticut and bears her state name-plate under her chin and at the nape of her neck. Homesick natives of Connecticut State constantly come up to her and, patting her lovingly on her hot muzzle, say, "Say, sister, I'm from Connetticut too. What's your hometown?" Then Stephanie regretfully, and with an acquired British accent, has to confess that she has naturalised as an alien.

Although so young, Stephanie has seen a great deal of life. She started from New York. When she started, we scarcely knew one knob on her figure from another, and the uses of almost all knobs were hidden from us. So we hired a man called Al to drive us down to Philadelphia, explaining the knob-psychology of Stephanie as he drove. Unfortunately Al proved to have an important engagement which dragged him from us just as we approached the outlying suburbs of Philadelphia and threw him into the New York train. We still had twenty miles to go. Stephanie sat smiling like a black devil where her faithless driver had left her. Since I had spent a longer time in the front seat than S. I now dubiously assumed the responsibility of driving. A Ford, we had been told, was fool-proof, and I was certainly a fool within the meaning of the act. I knocked a few knobs about— Stephanie moved.... Proudly hopeful that we were so far in no way distinguishable from the hundred million (or so) other Ford owners of the United States, we drove to Broad Street. We did not know the way to Radnor—our destination—but Broad Street looked a purposeful— almost a fool-proof—street. Rain streaked the wind-shield; all the outside world was a-dazzle and a-squirm seen through the glass. The darkness and the lights and the polished road were splintered in our confused sight. But still we moved successfully.

Something was wrong. I had committed a crime. Stephanie had committed a crime. Everyone in the world was shouting at us. Two policemen were running towards us gesturing insanely, each shouting something different out of one corner of his mouth.

"Say, where was you raised?"

"Say, can't you see the sign?"

"Say, when you gwineter wake up?"

Stephanie suddenly fainted and, as she did so, the position became dreadfully clear. In docile obedience to some nod, beck, or wreathed smile from a policeman, all the other automobiles going up and down Broad Street had stopped. Alone, Stephanie had proceeded innocently across an oasis of forbidden ground and now had fainted upon a tram-line, so that trams from two directions were blocked. Everyone in the world would be late for dinner. Nothing would move again. The block by now would be miles long. Back, way back, in Baltimore, in Washington, in San Francisco, in Honolulu ...people would be held up, cursing Stephanie. The business of the United States would be at a standstill. There would be international complications—another Great War....

"Well say, what's eating you? Step on her, can't you?"

"What do I step on, for God's sake?"

I stepped on everything. I tore everything from its socket except the hand-brake, which I left gripping Stephanie's vitals. Yet Stephanie awoke to the fact that she was fool-proof. She moved in a series of appalling spasms with a loud grinding noise. We were safe in a side

street before she fainted again. Collecting our fluttering wits suffi-
ciently to take off the brake at last, we rolled for two hours about the
wet trackless wastes of suburban Philadelphia, trying to find a way to
Radnor without crossing cruel Broad Street again. By a miracle we fell
over Radnor in the dark....

We know knobs better now. After that Stephanie took the matter
into her own hands and we could only sit in turns at her steering-wheel
and admire her spirit. She loved to leap ahead at thirty or forty miles
an hour, and once, passing a stout, road-filling Cadillac, she skidded in
soft gravel and bounded from the road into the virgin forests of Mary-
land. Only a very solid object can stop a highly-strung car like
Stephanie when her gasolene is up. In this case it was the trunk of a
fallen tree combined with the frenzied entreaties of her driver that re-
minded her of her duty. She sustained a cracked wind-shield and a
sprained head-light and had to put herself into the hands of a Ford sur-
geon.

Great minds, it is said—and said far too often—think alike, and
Stephanie found herself continually arriving in the same cities as
Maréchal Foch, who was at that time touring the States, receiving the
freedom of cities he probably intended never to visit again, and accept-
ing swords of honour which it is hoped the League of Nations will
never allow him to use. He had everything America could give him—
except a Ford. We saw him often, making shift with a Pierce Arrow,
whistling up excited main streets, pressed in with a full measure of
compressed military minions. I admit we never managed to pass
him—but then in the South no-one ever passes anyone. Everyone is
stuck in a bog all the time.

Upon the roads of North and South Carolina and of Georgia it is at
least an aesthetic pleasure to get bogged. The roads are the only vivid
things in the South. The colour of gumbo is a dazzling rust, sometimes
a bright vermilion. Gumbo is of a glue-like consistency, most useful in
its proper place—no doubt it would mend china or weld iron or add
body to chewing-gum; as the foundation of a highway, however, it
would disconcert a stronger character than Stephanie. There are always two ruts on a gumbo road. They are two feet deep or more, yet a
hardy Ford can flounder along them at a spanking three miles an hour,
until it meets another Ford floundering along in the opposite direction
on the same pair of ruts. Everyone then alights from both Fords and
sinks irritably into knee-high gumbo. The drivers argue for a while and
then he of the strongest character blithely helps the more pliable party

to heave the latter's Ford into the bottomless outer gumbo. Then there is weeping and gnashing of teeth until a cynical passing mule consents—for a consideration—to haul the unfortunate out. There is none of that romantic brotherhood-of-the-road stuff in the Carolinas.

There are tears in the air of that country in the winter, in spite of the persistent laughter of the negroes. The thin woods brood like rain-clouds; the cotton-fields are desolate and dripping, and untidy tufts of dirty white cotton still cling to the plants. Cotton was an unappreciated crop that year, and on all the waste places of the plantations were great bales of unsold cotton rotting in the rain. One saw cardinal birds sometimes—beads of flying fire—but they seemed to have no song. The only cheerful voices were those of the negroes; whole villages of negroes, it seemed, had nothing to do but laugh in cracked foolish voices. They laughed when they fell off their mules or when they went to church or when their buggies had to capsize in the ditches to make room for Stephanie or when they sold us new-laid eggs or asked us to what church we were affiliated or gave us wrong directions with expansive gestures.

Alabama, Mississippi and Louisiana are swamp states and all their trees are bearded with Spanish moss. To Southerners trees so festooned are, I suppose, as genial and domestic as ivied oaks are to us. But I think that this grisly grey lichen is one of the most mean and furtive-looking inventions of nature. My heart sinks now when I remember it; it seems to me the banner of a weeping land. That is the South that stays in my mind; New Orleans did not dispel the impression, nor brisk Atlanta, nor scholastic Athens high on a sunny hill. Even the memory of a two days' wait for the Mobile ferry at Daphne, a sunny windy village with a generous and radiantly humble little inn under great live-oak trees, a place with a silver beach sloping to the jade-grey Gulf of Mexico at its feet—remains an isolated memory.

New Orleans, as we saw it, could be simply described as a wet place surrounded by water.

Stephanie almost became an amphibian after she set wheel in Mississippi and Louisiana. She did not like it—and Stephanie is one of those who never suffer in silence. She had a hysterical trick of stopping dead with a horrifying coughing noise on the gang-planks of ferries at an angle of forty-five degrees. This she did in order to make her drivers appear fools in the eyes of ferrymen. We became familiar with the meaning silences of ferrymen as Stephanie settled down—a sheer derelict—upon their gang-planks. After an awkward silence the ferryman usually said, "Say, yu hevn't bin driving a Ford very long, I lay, hev yu?"

We then blushed deeply and said, "I guess there must be something wrong with a spark-plug or what not...."

The ferryman would then change his gum into the other cheek and get into the driver's seat of Stephanie who, at once, with a guttural roar of malicious amusement, slid faultlessly into her allotted place.

Sometimes the ferries on the way to New Orleans are quite sophisticated, and have crews consisting of as many as two men, and have funnels with real smoke coming out of them. Sometimes they are as primitive as Ed's ferry. Ed's ferry was a wooden "flat" towed by a limping gasolene launch along the channels of a desolate and malarial swamp in Louisiana. The launch contained Ed, and, on the flat, Stephanie and we were enthroned. Ed was a coloured gentleman who wore a bowler hat and a shiny serge "gents' city suiting", now worn from blue to mauve. He could earn, on his own admission, about twenty dollars a day, but was nevertheless aggrieved, apparently because he was obliged to get out of bed to ply his indolent trade. Fourteen miles we trailed limply after Ed along an airless *bayou* lined with swamp grass fifteen or twenty feet high. All the big trees in that dubious land were dead, killed, it seemed, by the spectral grey moss which hung in long wreaths and loops from the grey brittle branches. The trees had roots like snakes, writhing unhealthily in the black bog. The smaller trees had but a few more hopeful but fading leaves. There was nothing green in those sodden forests except the tray-like leaves of lilies on the water, and sometimes little low palms like hands among the tall rushes—like hands outstretched for the departed light of the sun. We saw nothing alive for two hours and a half, except some cranes and a hunter with a dead racoon on his back.

When we parted from Ed he gave us a pass for another ferry. He said he "didn't care to write", so we wrote our own pass and, at Ed's dictation, forged his name.

Another coloured gentleman drove us about New Orleans, up and down the old French quarter that must once have been so gay and is now so papery and squalid. The plaster is peeling from the frivolous old walls now, the trees are overgrown, the turned-back *jalousies* have lost their hinges and their trimness and their green French insolence. Jackson Square, where the first—but insufficiently advertised— Declaration of Independence in the United States took place in 1768, when the French returned, without thanks, a Spanish Governor to

78

Spain, still retains a certain faded stateliness, but its arcades, filled with dead rusted cannon, are boarded and railed up now.

Although of course the ubiquitous Maréchal Foch was still dogging the steps of Stephanie, and the city was gay with flags in spite of the rain, New Orleans seemed a drooping old widow of a city. Its glory seemed a glory of yesterday and was as meaningless to-day as rouge on an old cheek.

There were millionaires and movie palaces and sky-scrapers and oyster bars and bootleggers and Creole dancing dives; there was "uplift", as a result of which no fewer than five "probes" could be counted on the front page of one newspaper—every scandal reported with helpful completeness. There was a city park with improved Greek architecture in it. And the old Spanish fort, a crumbling mound of yellow-red brick, crowned with tipsy-looking old cannon, was now the centre of a "Fun City" with a switchback and popcorn booths and a Great Wheel, and nothing lacking that could possibly help to keep an old Spanish fort in countenance. These things were like a gaudy veil upon a fine dead face.

When the elect of the city die in these days, they go to the bristling cemetery, of which an acre or two is, one gathers, doubly consecrated for the use of millionaires. The tombs of the millionaires, our guide assured us, cost anything up to a quarter of a million dollars. He pointed out that they were real elegant, and that some of them were lighted up by electricity every night to match the movie halls and the all-night dives outside—so that, even in the dark, God might not overlook the fact that there were millionaires waiting there to whom expense was no object.

Every traveller moves in a world of prophecies, and we were told by nearly everyone we met that we should never get out of Louisiana into Texas. There were stretches of road that were vouched for as impassable, and their names will always bring back to me the feeling of desperate and black defiance with which we approached them. A great many of the country people in Louisiana are French, and those we met had very small hearts and very hungry purses. The roads were said to be deliberately kept impassable by the French farmers near them. The farmers stood with their mules all day near bog-holes that could have been filled in with a couple of cart-loads of stones and a little good-will. Like vultures, the farmers flocked to devour the derelict cars in the holes. They haggled for their price—five dollars a pull—before they would hook their chains. Hats off to thrift.

But in the end we crossed over into kind sandy Texas, and left prophets and profiteers behind us for a while.

The desert met us quite suddenly beyond San Antonio. Suddenly there were no more sugar plantations, there was no more tobacco; suddenly the trees disappeared and mountains sprang out of the strangling swamp—strange mountains with flat summits like martello towers. The prickly pears were of all shades of red and green. The hills were of pale rock covered with a low leafless scrub. Our Ford's wheels were set sometimes on white boulder-ledges, sometimes in the waters of little clear gay rivers which impudently crossed our path and were innocent of bridges; mostly we ran uneasily on sand. There were bump-gates across the trail to keep one rancher's steers from another's. A bump-gate is opened by the car itself—with some damage to the mud-guards. You have simply to collide with one wing of the gate with exactly the right amount of force. If you bump too hard the other wing of the gate spins round and damages your back mudguard; if you bump too tenderly nothing happens—the gate remains shut. The secret is a simple one when once learnt, and I consider it curious that no steer on record has ever been able to defeat the ends of man by mastering it.

After a thousand miles of travelling over desert, partly through deep soft sand, partly over naked rock, partly through shallow *arroyos*, always along a trail defined only by more or less meagre ruts and by stumps and stones blazed with the colours of our trail, Stephanie developed nervous breakdowns. A Ford of her aristocratic temperament might well suffer from such experiences. There were times when she had no cosy gasolene-smelling garage to sleep in at night, when all night long she had to stand, the centre of a very amateur camp, and listen to the screams of the coyotes and watch the shooting stars leap from one horizon to the other; there were times when even the horizon might be known by heart without looking, and when destinations never seemed to come nearer, even after days of travel. In parts of Texas only one design in mountains is turned out; the slopes of these standardised eminences are all at one angle, and the summits are as flat as though cut out in paper with one stroke of the scissors. Both mountain and desert are covered with one neutral colour, and there are no surprises—except the cowboys.

When I was about ten I was so unmaidenly as to announce publicly my intention of marrying a cowboy. Years have brought me reticence and the sad discovery that all ideals are very shy game—yet years have not changed my enthusiasm for the heroic genus about

80

which the arts of Messrs. Bret and William S. Hart(e) are built. The cowboys are the real flowers of the desert. Those of the ordinary public who have seen the movies may clothe the cowboys of their secret romances forever in the bright colours that used to constitute their gala wear. At a rodeo in California, six years ago, the cowboys proved themselves capable of wearing, without a trace of bashfulness, scarlet shirts, orange neckerchiefs, yellow sombreros, and crimson wool chaps. Cowboys on the everyday desert, however, favour protective colouring—unless they are Mexican. In any of the rather dust-coloured little towns of south-west Texas—towns that are flung upon the desert without apparent reason, blown, one would say, to their locations by the indifferent desert wind that blows nobody either good or ill—the cowboys swagger up and down in modest leather or sheep-skin waistcoats and flapping leather chaps; their only touch of dandyism is shown in their high boots, stitched in floral designs, and in their tall broad desert-coloured hats. Gorgeous colours are out of fashion, even on holidays. At a rodeo in El Paso all the splendour was concentrated on gold-and silver-studded saddles, cuff-bands and belts.

The end of a rodeo always leaves me vowing that the thing is as cruel as bullfighting and that I will never witness such a conflict again. The beginning of the next rodeo, however, finds me seated eagerly on the nearest available bench, busy persuading myself that calves love being roped from a distance and tied in knots, that bulls enjoy the feeling of having their necks twisted by bull-dozers until their legs fail them, and that it does young men good to fall crashing from the upper air into which they have been shot from the humped backs of frantic broncos.

Cowboys are a sort of madness with me because they seem to belong so slightly to-day. Swagger is as much part of the cowboy's equipment as it was that of the soldier of fortune of yesterday. There is nothing damping to me about the fact that their swagger is largely self-conscious and deliberate. All that is in keeping with their old splendid swashbuckling rôle. The fact that in these days they occasionally arrive in their characteristic cloud of dust, not on a bronco pulled up from a full gallop at the door, but in a Ford car, is only slightly disappointing. A Ford—a cowboy's Ford—can jingle, can prance, can be jerked, foaming, to its haunches. Ford or bronco, the cowboy glitters still in a halo of spurs and boastings and sixshooters.

We heard a cowboy at Sonora remarking—in order to be overheard—that he drawed the line at nothing but horse-stealing. His neighbour obviously thought that this would make an almost Sunday-school impression on the public, so he hastened to add that he himself was not above riding a horse he "didn't know the owner of". They watched our faces. All their talk was swagger, and they were quite certain of our credulity and admiration and of that of the young lady chewing gum behind the counter of the "caife".

Young women in the West simper to match the men's swagger. Sombreroed beauties who ride gloriously from one adventure to another have never been seen by me in the Western States—indeed, I know no Western girls who can sit a horse at all. As far as I have seen the young generation of Western charmers, they seem to be exclusively indoor. Pioneering was mother's job. With rouge, rolled silk stockings, near-silk jumpers, hobble-skirts and silly pretty little city toques, they outrage the enormous desert skies; on high French heels they totter along remote boardwalks; with servile squeakings and gigglings and nudgings they ensnare the simple cowboy hearts that we have believed that only the free, the untamed, the primeval, the trick-equestrienne female—(like us in our movie mood)—could ever charm or deserve. Here are mincing suburban morals, small-town graces, city smirks and wiles, seducing our interesting rogues....

It is most disheartening for those of us who try so hard to be good yet attractive to see how easy it is for rogues to make their effect. We good mild persons who powder our noses and pin our hopes to marriage with a docile bread-winner—we are inheriting and devastating the earth. We have invented Disarmament and Prohibition and the Girl Guide Movement and Higher Thought—and lo! one splendid lie, one fantastic coxcomb, can make us all look fools!

At the joining of three exotic lands—Texas, New Mexico and Mexico proper—here perhaps will be the last stronghold of swagger and sombreros. Surely for a long time yet Mexico will be naughty, will be uninfected by the spirit of the movies and of ice-cream sodas and of Harold Bell Wright. Juarez, on the Mexican side of the Rio Grande, opposite El Paso, has, it is refreshing to learn, ninety-seven saloons and one soda-fountain.

Stephanie went into Mexico. Indeed, she broke down in the soft sand of a Mexican street. There is more provision for the reviving of men than of motor-cars in Juarez, and Stephanie, having fainted for lack of gasolene, had difficulty in finding a garage to supply her. Her drivers, on the other hand, had difficulty in walking a step in any direction without being offered stimulants.

Mexicans may be backward in many ways; their adobe houses give no hint of progress or hygiene, the children in their streets are hardly cleaner or less forlorn than the pariah dogs, soldiers slouch along as furtively as thieves, the solitary visible policeman of Juarez droops, limply yawning, against a hitching post all day with his uniform unbuttoned. But in taking advantage of the opportunity presented by the proximity of an enormous thirsty neighbour like the United States, Mexicans have not been at all slow. Nobody seems to think of the border of Mexico now as a lawless region which wise men avoid; on the contrary, the very mention of it makes the average mouth water. I should not be surprised to hear that quite a considerable percentage of the hundred million inhabitants of the United States is making discreet enquiries at real estate offices in search of properties as near as possible to a land so richly flowing with milk and honey—(to put it rather euphemistically).

It is possible that this trend of "Hundred-per-cent Americans" towards the Mexican border may have a civilising missionary effect on Mexico. But it is not very probable, if one may judge from two days spent between saloon and saloon among American civilisers in Mexico.

The desert showed itself more and more austerely to us every day. Sometimes the deep soft sand entrapped us and we had to work really hard to escape. The desert was never flat, never so simple as it looked, never bare. Fantastic mountains surrounded us always, and cactuses became more riotous and more incredible as we crossed New Mexico towards Arizona. In Arizona occurs the culmination of the crescendo of cactuses. Sajuaros are everywhere; they point at the sky in such numbers that broad hillsides seem like steepled cities. The sajuaro must be a standing joke among the more conventional kindly fruits of the earth. The fact that it stands more or less describes it—an upright green corrugated hirsute thing with a waist-measurement of perhaps fifty inches. It is waist all the way down. It looks like someone who has lost his hat. It stands anywhere between twenty and thirty feet high. Sometimes the more imaginative sajuaros produce one or two absurd little crooked fingers, corrugated and hairy like the main stem, pointing idiotically this way and that. I have often felt that by standing up to a sajuaro and insulting it and then stabbing it through and through its fat green ribs till the tip of one's quivering blade came out through the other side, one would have all the thrill of being a murderer without its disadvantages. There is a fatter and even sillier cactus that sits at the feet of the sajuaro. It resembles those round cushions on which some people sit by the fire in drawing-rooms. It cannot, however, be used for the same purpose, since it is very prickly. There is a brown cactus like a splash of rigid snakes, and there is another which pathetically tries to beautify itself by wearing a few thick stalkless yellow flowers on its angular and whiskered knuckles. But the sajuaros command the scene, and when I think of them I am again waking up at dawn, lying on the sand, facing a crack of rising sun behind the square-topped mountains, and the long simple shadows of the sajuaros lie across the lilac-grey slopes.

One night, on a switchback mountain track, fifteen miles short of the next town, gasolene ran short. There was some gasolene, to be sure, in Stephanie's tank, enough to carry us for miles over a flat road. But gasolene, even in a fool-proof Ford, must submit to the laws of natural science, and, when a tank is tilted insanely backward up grades that only an aeroplane could calmly tackle, gasolene simply will not flow forward. We stuck in a dry river bed. With a take-off from soft sand, Stephanie could not be induced to surmount the high very steep bouldery bank on the farther side. We had been warned never to camp in dry river-beds. A shower in some distant high valley might make such a camp a death trap. But Stephanie vowed she would camp nowhere else that night, unless gasolene was supplied. I had an idea. I know now from whom that idea came, but at the time I wafted thanks for it in the wrong direction. I had noticed that gasolene always floats on the surface of water. I thought, "If we fill our tank half full of water, the gasolene will be lifted up to the level of the pipe and so we shall be saved." Perhaps I shall not be believed when I say that to a certain point this idea worked. Stephanie, with her spirit thus uplifted by water from a pool of the river, reached the top of the bank. And there she died.

Among the cactuses on a tiny plateau a tinker had made his camp. He had two donkeys and two little idiot sons. It was what is called a family of "white trash" travelling from Kentucky to the State of Washington. But trash though the tinker might be, he was not unfriendly to us—offered us the use of his fire—(firewood in cactus country is hard to find)—offered us bacon—mumbled mildly to us. Screened from the light of his fire by steeples of sajuaro, we unrolled our blankets, and only awoke next morning to see the tinker rattling away with his donkeys and his kettles and his little cackling boys. We asked him to get help for us when he should reach town, but the vacant look on his face did not encourage us to hope. So S. presently set out on a fifteen mile walk, and Stephanie and I sat hoping we might see a bear—at a reasonable distance. Nothing, however, happened for some hours, and then a car, carrying S. and some strangers from Montana, arrived.

"Why, look who's here!" said the chief gentleman from Montana, speaking out of Stephanie's digestive organs. "You got water in yer tank."

We said no word.

"It's these gararges—they're all as slick'n crooked as they can be these days. If a guy looks kinda green these gararges'll hold him up for his bottom cent...."

We said no word.

The kind man from Montana let the water out of Stephanie's tank and gave us enough gasolene to take us to the next town. He left us still green but grateful. Even more green and more grateful than we gave him to suppose.

The town of Benson—grand old name—came next to the town of Tombstone—and all on the way to Death Valley. This ill-conceived sequence seemed to us like a disturbing hint from a better world— almost as alarming as angels calling. We decided to pass through Benson and Tombstone with faces averted; we swore that we would not even buy a pint of gasolene or a sardine in either, and that we would shun Death Valley. For ten days I had been a wreck owing to some accident in the middle ear, caused by constant jolting, which left me so violently giddy that I could at no time stand without support, and sometimes could not even sit upright. At a hotel in El Paso we had been refused a room, probably because I gave the impression that I had already called at all the ninety-seven saloons of Juarez. Deming, New Mexico, in spite of the 99 per cent purity which inspires its boosting slogan, found me reeling and rolling still. As for the really beautiful steep rusty city of Bisbee, Arizona, its high vivid mountains whirl and swing upon my memory like great waves of the sea. I was convinced that if we stopped at Benson, near Tombstone, I should die. To have one's name coupled with a tombstone was the same as to have one foot in the grave. We tore through Tombstone; we burst through Benson. Tombstone tried to lassoo us in the noose of a strong icy wind. We turned up our collars and drove on. Benson tried to hold us in a bog. We overcame the bog. Both tried to threaten us by means of a most ominous low red smoky sky. We refused to be impressed. And then—

BENSON

this in the southernmost desert seemed the ultimate surprise, the most refined form of treachery—snowflakes were seen to fall and vanish on Stephanie's hot nose, and the next minute a blizzard had wrapped us up. Our purpose was snatched out of our hands and whirled away on the giddy white choking wind. We tried faithfully to drive on. We did drive on until we were two Lot's wives. And then we had to give up. In fact we had to make such an effort to get back to Benson, that Benson for a while became a hope instead of a fear. That, it seemed to me, was the wiliness of unescapable fate. We spent the night in Benson in a house of gloomy smells. I brooded on death—ah, it was cruel, I seemed so young to die.... I remembered various flaws in my will. My life, I now saw, had been full of errors and imperfections. I slept feverishly, listening for the rustle of wings. I awoke absolutely cured of all ills. We paid the overcharges of the landlady like a happy ransom. I could hardly eat my fried egg for singing—and it was a bad one.

Stephanie almost lost heart on the border of Arizona and California. There was no limit to the demands that were put upon her, and the imprint of her terrible experiences will never be erased from her countenance. She reached California a prematurely-aged Ford; rheumatism and asthma were among the least of her complaints; at one time she actually became delirious; her horn began to blow by itself, and continued to make itself heard in senseless ravings for a stretch of about twenty miles. This sad condition, so unlike that of the sparkling and frolicsome young Ford who left Connecticut two months before, almost brought tears to the eyes of her drivers. But nobody could wonder at it. In the space of the last ten days of the journey Stephanie was wrapped in snow, drowned in floods, parched on a ninety-five mile stretch of desert so bare and comfortless that, according to one informant, even the "jack-rabbits carried their lunches with them", and, in the end, cooled and diamonded with spray from a pearly sunset sea.

Crossing from Arizona we almost lost hope. At one moment, if an obliging aeroplane had offered us a lift, we might have abandoned Stephanie and accepted. The Colorado river had flooded miles of roads about eighteen inches deep in water. The water devilishly concealed the lapses in the road, and one day we only travelled eighteen miles—working hard from sunrise to sunset—wallowing out of one muddy crisis into another. At every mud-hole we had to wade back and forth to the nearest point of dry land with our kit in order to lighten the car, we had to chop sticks and, bending double, elbow-deep in opaque wa-

86

ter, thrust them under Stephanie's spinning, splashing wheels. We had lost our tyre-chains in a bottomless mud-hole. Also we had another loss. Money in an inner coat pocket is safe enough in circumstances that permit a man to stand dry and upright as his Maker intended him to stand. But tip that man in and out of a Ford foundering in floods, load him with wet kit-bags, bend him like a hairpin, bereave him of hope and dignity—and where is that money at the end of the day? Where indeed is it? We had nothing now but a few dollars, which I found, sodden, in my breeches pocket. Would a pigskin case of greenbacks and Cook's cheques float? I waded back a mile, barefoot on the soft slimy mud beneath the water, to see if money would float. But money is specially designed to be elusive. It either rolls or sinks. S., disabled by short sight from joining in the watery search, stripped Stephanie to the last tin of corned-beef, building a castle of kit-bags, coats, cameras, cans, and pans on an island in the flood. The money was nowhere; there is nothing so thoroughly lost as lost money. Poor S., waiting gloomily for my return, sitting in the reloaded car, had to bear further injury. A Ford-full of cowboys ploughing through the water, having passed me knee-deep in flood and despair "way back", stopped to tell S. what chivalrous America thinks of monocled Englishmen who sit in dry ease in opulent Fords while their wives wade barefoot behind. Poor S.'s protests were not understood, except as a further aggravation. The English tongue as we understand it is not spoken in the enlightened West.

Ah, chivalrous America.... Arriving that evening at a small cheerless hamlet, cold, soaked and exhausted, we were given a room full of holes, through which the draughts whistled. The place was cold as— chivalry. We were soaked, shivering, and sad. One hole in the floor showed us the store beneath, and to the store we went, to sit on the counter by the stove and seek sympathy. We told our host and the assembled cowboys of the loss of our money, and a kind of auction followed, the chivalrous cowboys and storekeeper haggling for the highest possible proportion of the lost money to be paid to the finder. When this generous rivalry had reached its most expensive point, two or three sympathisers went off to look for the money. Whether they found it or not, only they can tell. *We* never saw it again.

The remaining cowboys sat in a row on the counter, eating bananas, and—with a chilling effect of bathos—discussing the various makes and prices of cowboy clothes. I asked them if I might sketch them. They were as much pleased as flappers, and they meticulously called my attention to the particular glories of their outfits. They were so anxious to watch the progress of the drawing, and at the same time to maintain their noble poses, that they almost broke themselves in two. Each man thought the drawing of his neighbour "dandy", but each was ashamed of the portrait of himself. One man was much offended to find that his *mustache* was not perceptibly included in the group.

Next morning, as we started through the floods again, a cowboy rode splashing after us to ask if he might have the sketch of himself for his mother. But it was deep in a kit-bag; we were English and unchivalrous, and we had had enough of submarine unpacking.

Although we had now almost no money, we had the first gesture of a stroke of luck. We found a beautiful new tyre—no Ford's property, but the lost darling of a Pierce Arrow. It filled nearly the whole of Stephanie's seating space. Perhaps a large reward would be offered—enough to take us to San Francisco. Perhaps the millionaire owner would never think of it again, and we—after a decent interval of uncertainty—would turn our treasure into gold. At any rate there was a kind of perfume of relief about that tyre. We drove proudly up to the next garage.

"Anybody missed a tyre?"

"Nary a one, sister. It's a dandy one, too. Worth money."

"If nobody claims it or reports it, d'you think we could sell it? We've lost nearly all our money."

"Sure you could sell it...."

But we couldn't, for next morning it was gone. The garage mechanic said he had given it away to a man. "I guess he was the owner all right." We guessed he wasn't. There was a terrible scene. We had built hopes on that tyre. The shock of the fall of our hopes made us tremble with rage. The garage man said, "See here, strangers, let me tell you, you gotta lot to learn about America ... us big-hearted Westerners, we don't want no money for doing a neighbour a good turn...." But this rococo pedestal was easily demolished. There was nothing for us to do except frighten the man and make him look a fool, and this we did with a whole heart. He had stolen our treasure and our last hope. In a moment he offered us money to say no more. He was really frightened when we refused and left him, the word *sheriff* on our lips. But we had no time to seek justice. We must hurry to Los Angeles, racing with our shrinking resources.

There can be few experiences that equal the journey across the desert from Blythe, on the Colorado river, to Mecca, on the Salton Sea, and thence across the San Gorgonio Pass into a plain brimming with orange groves, bristling with palms and the languid spires of eucalyptus.

From the desert one descends into the red mouth of a canyon which winds darkly and grotesquely through mountains. At every turn of the trail—which is nothing more than the sandy bed of an old dead river—one thinks that one has fallen into a trap of the gods. There is, it seems, no way out—yet suddenly a narrower passage still, at a sharp angle, catches the seeker's eye and leads him on. And so one gropes incredulously on until one comes out abruptly into sunlight and into sight of a great view of the dead salt sea, 200 feet below sea-level—a leaden lake bound in ashen banks of alkali. And behind it the tall snow mountains leap into the sky.

Los Angeles is a sophisticated city; it has no eccentricities and no heart. It is approached through oil-fields that tower in skeleton groups like thin enormous dead forests. There could be no charming adventures in Los Angeles, I think, even in that crimped silly suburb, Hollywood, where they turn out adventures ready-made. Yet there was treasure for us in Los Angeles—treasure of a kind. We sold the fag-end of our insurance back to its issuing company for some useful hard dollars. And so—San Francisco at last, that kind odd northern California that smiles among mists and flowers and honest winds between the hills and the sea.

Of those forty-six hundred miles now there is nothing, it seems, left to us. The miles are packed in concentrated tabloid form in the speedometer of Stephanie, and in a couple of diaries which we shall perhaps never look at again. The print of our tyres, the charred ghosts of our camp-fires are buried deep in sand and lost now. The things we do run out like water or sand between our fingers. Truly travellers are fools to open their arms so wide and to possess so little in the end.

THE STATES AGAIN—II

These are some of the little midges of seeing and hearing that are caught in the spider-web of my memory at the end of that struggle across a continent.

Henderson, North Carolina—Health Hustle Henderson—reached on Thanksgiving Day. I remember noticing at dinner how full of secret understanding the restaurant was, what an undercurrent of meaning flowed beneath each order, how effective were desires that never found expression, and what suggestive-looking liquid substances were brought by waiters in opaque glasses and cups in obedience to cries for innocent things like milk, coffee, lemonade with a dash of maple syrup.... As strangers we knew no passwords and as aliens we had no excuse to Give Thanks. Late that night on our landing we fell over the powerless form of one whose thanks had been given in full measure, a Hundred-Per-Cent American for whom the claims of God and the Pilgrim Fathers very logically took precedence of the decrees of Mr. Volstead.

I remember the first time we camped, near Grover, South Carolina. A soft rain fell on us through the branches of a little wood, and the light of Stephanie's head-lights cut dramatically out of the blackness of the wood branches and twigs and leaves hung with beads of rain. The frogs roared in the rain, and on the distant road we could hear the voices of ordinary domestic people going home. We felt like a very important secret in our iron strongbox of rain and the shouting of frogs—our safe, clamped with the jointed steel bars of trees.

I remember King's Mountain City's welcoming sign, "Go slow and see our city, go fast and see our jail." And the sign in a grocer's store in Georgia, "If you spit at home, spit here, make yourself at home."

I remember that in Montgomery as we stopped Stephanie, a young man threw his arm affectionately round S.'s shoulders. "Say, listen, you need a raincoat," he said. I thought him an unusually kind and confident weather-prophet, perhaps a professional Greeter employed by the city council of Montgomery to welcome strangers and warn them of the vagaries of the local weather. But S. was more suspicious; he drew himself up haughtily; this, he suspected, was some idiom new to him and had almost certainly an insolent inner meaning. "What's the joke?" said S. coldly. "Joke—not on your life. I say you need a rain-coat—'s'plain American. I k'n let you have the best raincoat on the market—the Never-mind Raincoat—fourteen dollars'n worth four times as much...."

I remember the daughter of the kind landlady at Richmond, Texas. The daughter was a heartless but faultless pianist, an interpreter of Chopin and Mendelssohn after a style which those composers could scarcely have foreseen. For she played them with perfect fluency—*but always jazzed.* She could not conceive of an unsyncopated rhythm. We were happy in Richmond, Texas. There the badlands, at last, were no longer swamp and damp sugar-cane—they were red prairies, like a sunset pressed and dried in a big book.

I remember camping on Christmas Eve near Sonora, Texas, and, ranging along a stream-bank in search of firewood, disturbing a row of little turtles so that with one impulse they dived from their log, pricking an accurate neat line of perforations in the water.

We had our Christmas luncheon in the shade of a great prickly pear with crimson and golden discs. And as we cooked our Christmas bacon on sticks in the flame, a big furry animal, with black horizontal stripes from grey shoulder to ringed tail, crossed a near space at a lumbering short-legged run, its heavy coat swinging on its back.

I remember a dirty kind hotel in Balmorrhea—(a name which somehow sounds like taking the name of Queen Victoria in vain)— and the deep cavey lake of Phantom Springs, just outside Balmorrhea, and the embarrassing stare of the overdressed prudish black furry cattle as we bathed.

I remember sitting nearly all day in a garage in Los Angeles while Stephanie was being overhauled, having an argument about God with some very pleasant intelligent mechanics, ex-cavalrymen from the Philippines.

I remember being stuck for want of gasolene at night on the top of a high Californian mountain road, and being found by a very good Samaritan who was short of gasolene himself but gave us enough to enable us to reach the long grade down which we could slide on our own weight. Not content with this, he followed us conscientiously in his car to make sure that we reached the valley safely. And at the bottom of the hill I remember the Holy City, headquarters of some cult called the P.C.D.W.—the meaning of the initials is secret. They sell rose-jam there and texts and fantastic pamphlets praising—if I remember right—man above God and woman above man. But their theories, which were locally reported to be subversive and dangerous, did not spoil their coffee and their kindness at midnight to stranded aliens.

I remember the almost unbearable excitement of driving at last up the drive of the best of friends between orchards in the Santa Clara valley, which is almost more lovely than home to me. *Yes ... they haven't gone to bed yet ... look at the light ... look at the log fire ... he's reading aloud to her.... Now they've heard us.... They'll wonder.... Now they're running out....*

THE STATES AGAIN—III

We got stuck in a bog in California—four of us in Stephanie. It was a particularly black and pervasive bog and, after three hours of splashing and wallowing among levered planks, we reached dry land looking like the submerged tenth. It was late and we went to a little wooden inn in a Spanish village. When we had knocked for some time, the proprietor awoke and opened the door.

"Rooms for de night ... sure, step right in...." He raised the candle to our varnished bebogged faces. "Ah yuss ... why ... dat's as may be ... step right out again, folks, you k'n sleep on de floor in, de annex, ef you want ... dere's five udder coloured coons dere—jazz entertainers—dey'll make room fer you."

And so they did, and sang very sweetly over their breakfast next day, too.

THE STATES AGAIN—IV

The Grand Canyon of the Colorado river in Arizona is the only object in creation that cannot possibly be coldly or superciliously seen. I wonder, in passing, whether the word *creation* can be properly used of the Canyon. Rather it is an interruption in the order of created things. Here is a desert, as flat and everyday and conventional as any desert can be; it is moulded in cream-coloured sand and spotted with chaparral and low trees and white poppies; mirage lakes shimmer in gold and blue on its horizon. As a desert, in fact, it is aggressively orthodox, the eye travels serenely across Arizona towards equally serene Utah, when suddenly—Good God, what has happened? There is no desert—the desert has fallen through the world into hell—here is nothing but blue air perforated by blood-red towers. Gashed by chasm within chasm, the world crashes down, from midday into twilight, from twilight into night.

The desert is betrayed; it is revealed as no desert at all, but the broadest mountain peak in the world; it is slung up under the sky more than a mile above sea-level—and here the cords of the sky have broken, the desert has fallen. There is nothing higher except the sky; in the chasm the peaks and the pyramids, the pillars and the towers and the terrible scarred temples, though four or five thousand feet high themselves, never dare to rise above the rim of the tall false desert.

Here is the calm level of Arizona and, thirteen miles away, on the other side of chaos, Utah takes up the calm line of desert again as though eternity had never intervened.

What an inconceivably, ridiculously large snare for the feet of men the Canyon must have seemed to the first pioneers.

Shorty was an exquisite desert dandy with a very broad Mexican hat, yellow shirt, leather sleeveless coat, black neckerchief, flaring leather chaps buckled with silver, and high prettily stitched boots.

Once in his hands we put ourselves on the hooves of mules, and so we descended into the Canyon. Directly we had slipped over the rim it seemed as if—death being certain either way—it would be both quicker and cheaper to jump on foot over the 4000-feet cliffs. But Mommer robbed us of the expression of this thought. She was an elderly lady in a feathered picture hat and divided skirts, and she screamed without ceasing. Not one of us dared to murmur in competition with Mommer. Shorty was unmoved by her screams and addressed her with facetious coquetry. When—since she refused to move—he roped her mule to his and dragged her away, someone at the tail of the party shouted, "What about the Rape of the Sabines?" To Mommer we owe our dignity during two hair-raising days.

Our mules are the heroes of the story. They walked firmly and modestly down practically perpendicular places, rocks fell upon them, paths gave way beneath them, the thousandfold echoes of Mommer's braying made their ears twitch—yet they walked tranquilly on air and clouds and unpropped shadows, meditatively chewing dry thorns. Now and then Shorty, who rode ahead, would turn and whistle. At once we would find ourselves joggling in ignominious and terrifying haste towards him, like sheep after a shepherd, like trucks after an engine. Our stirrups, hanging, as it seemed, parallel with the mules' necks, clattered about their cynical ears.

The mad angular shapes of the peaks within the Canyon rose, and their colours were intensified, as we sank. There were scarlets and crimsons and blood-reds and plum-purples and cream-yellows and blinding whites, all built up in an infinite arrangement of buttressed horizontal lines. There was a glaze—a radiance of flowers at our feet, and there were patches of snow, poised like angels on the tips of stone needles far above and behind us. Finally there was the river, set in an ultimate night-dark cleft of which only the lips were visible from the rim.

No horizontal lines here, no reminders of the work of men's hands, no scarlets or gay yellows, no flowers. We rode down into shadow, into a geological whirlpool of still wild shapes and lines. At the foot of those stormy cliffs, far from sunlight and flowery silence, far below the feet of the fantastic red cathedrals and obelisks and pyramids, the Colorado river roared.

Between rapids it ran as smoothly as though under glass, and only the little errant sticks on its surface betrayed its frightful swiftness. In the rapids there were tall dragons of water, they tossed their golden manes and wings, and never bowed their heads. There were deserts of smooth indrawn water between these crested waves, there were varied levels separated by deep, hinted rocks and by scarred ridges of yellow foam. The geography of this dreadful kingdom of screaming water never changes.

We slept in a camp at the foot of an Olympic conception of the Flat-iron Building, New York City, 3000 feet high and done in carmine red.

Next day we rode twenty-three miles, fifteen along the edge of the dark cliff that leaned over the river—yet still, ourselves, 4000 feet below the rim. Glimpses of the ghostly pale river shot up, as it were, through gashes in the cliff. Now and then, where a rare cool stream made a little oasis of grass and clover and bright poplar trees in the waste of sandy chaparral and cactus, we paused and straightened our creaking limbs. About us the pinnacles and peaks were like cactuses in stone. Even Mommer was silent as we climbed towards the rim again by a new and even steeper trail. To tremble, one felt, might disturb the superhuman balance of one's mule. The trail was threaded like a cord through niches and little tunnels in the sheer cliff. The blue shadows of sunset pursued us; as we rose, the drowning wild Canyon sank into a sea of blue shadow.

It seemed outrageous—after our tense and dreamlike two days among huge striding coloured stone shadows—to find tourists on the rim in tight skirts and city suits, still cackling through telescopes, still buying "postals", still thrilling with delicious alarm at the loud wardance of the sophisticated and peaceful Hopi Indians who lived opposite the hotel. Even Mommer had a halo of gorgeous experience. Even Mommer was withdrawn behind the veil of a remembered miracle. And though we too might wait our turn at the telescope, though we too might spend hours turning round the "dumb waiter" that displayed picture postcards, though we too might sit on Navajo rugs, thrilling as we dodged the whooping swoopings of naturally peacefully inclined Indians—yet we were aloof, it seemed, upon a pedestal of yesterday—nobody could mistake *us* for tourists....

"Animals and primitive people always know ..." we said to ourselves. Joe Yellowfeet, the most active Hopi Indian, showed himself a friend of ours. He honoured us often by shaking hands with us while still gasping from his war-dance. Sometimes we met him and his relations with vermilion stripes across their noses, with red feathers sticking up round their heads like a park-fence and swinging down their backs, with beaded buckskin coats and frilled leather trousers and heavy moccasins. At other times we found ourselves bowed to by exquisite young men in tight-waisted "jazz" tweeds, and only after a momentary check recognised the handsome if rather flattened physiognomy that distinguishes the aristocratic Yellowfeet family.

Rightly are Indians known as the vanishing race. Joe, like most other fine wild animals, knows how to vanish by taking refuge in protective colouring.

THE STATES AGAIN—V

The San Francisco-Chicago train made us conspicuous by stopping especially for our benefit in the middle of the night. On the platform there was no lamp, but a ray from one lighted shack dimly showed a sullen Indian face—a face inspired by no eagerness to help us to lift our property out of the train. But still in our minds was comfort and tranquillity, born of the advertisement that had brought us here—a promise of a hotel with twenty-four bedrooms and a regular motor service to Acoma, sixteen miles away. The soft obstinate darkness of the desert must be a mistake, we thought—a misprint upon our minds' retina; cups of hot coffee and rooms full of good beds beamed serenely in our hopes.

"Aw say ..." sympathetically said the lady telegraphist in the lighted shed. "Who's bin handing you that speel? There ain't no hotel anywheres this side of Alberkerky. There's a shack with an Indian dame in it, but her man's away and she's scared of strangers. You can't get to Acoma to-morrow neether—'nless you hike. Well say, ain't that too bad...."

She was a kind woman, but had no power over circumstances. I have often wondered what her life was and what she ate and whom she loved—apparently alone by a little lamp in a black desert.

We found the Indian dame's shack, a blacker indefinite mass in indefinite blackness. We knocked till the house shook and, after a long time, in a crack of the narrowly opened door, a woman appeared, wrapped in a red blanket, her thick plaits of black hair hanging forward over her crouching shoulders.

She was afraid of us. Her fear gave us a kind of bandit feeling and I put my foot in the crack of the door. This frightened her still more. "No room, no room ... twenty men here.... All bed fill up...."

After cooing like doves for a while without effect, we pushed in. We selected the cleanest of the dirty bedrooms.

Once we came into the light the woman was hypnotised by S.'s monocle. I don't know whether it made us seem more or less dangerous than she had expected. But it conquered her.

So at least the night was negotiated. But even the kind light of day, making steady torches of the bleak yellow *mesas* and polishing the pale surface of the desert, could not bridge over the sixteen miles to Acoma. Acoma was a place we had come far to see. Could we telephone to Albuquerque for a car? The kind lady in the depot shack was lamentably replaced by two very unamiable Indian men with faces like irritated horses. They would not even take their feet off the table to show us how the telephone worked. A ring at the telephone only produced replies in an unknown tongue. Vague memories of Fenimore Cooper did not supply us with the aboriginal translation of—"A Ford car, please, and look sharp about it ..."

We returned disconsolate to our Indian hostess. There was a smart little Dodge car outside her door. In the house were Gilbert and Beebo eating fried eggs. They introduced themselves. Both, I think, must have been partly Indian. Beebo was dressed like a cowboy—except for gentlemanly gaiters; Gilbert wore a dainty check suiting and seemed to be a travelling salesman. To us he sold nothing—except the only thing we wished to buy, a sight of Acoma.

It was good, after the hours of despair during which our feet had almost taken root in the desert sand, to feel wheels going round beneath us and to see the *mesas* coming closer. Good, but not comfortable. Rocks, cactuses, dry river-beds, dead coyotes, acres of tangled chaparral and bottomless sand—all these were no obstacle to Gilbert and Beebo.

Mesa Incantada—the enchanted *mesa*—was on our left, and Beebo was ready with the story. The *mesa* towered above us, a coffin two hundred feet high; it had no slopes, only vertical cliffs holding up a flat plane against the sky. But once there was a way up, Beebo said—only nobody knew how long ago. Indians, it seems, remember everything but dates. There was an Indian tribe up there—a very prosperous tribe, since no one could reach them to beat them in battle. But they were beaten all the same. An earthquake destroyed their stairway. They were imprisoned two hundred feet above the world—starving, with all the kindly coloured world at their feet.

"Acoma folks say their ghosts and their devils yell around up there on dark nights," said Beebo. "Dunno if it's true. Anyways, I often heardum ..."

"Some guy climbed up there one time and there was their houses, sure 'nough, and their dead bones," Gilbert added.

Acoma is built on a *mesa* just the same shape, but it isn't a coffin, for Acoma lives and thrives. The Dodge car drew up at the foot of a long dune of sand blown against the yellow cliff. The flat little yellow houses of Acoma look like machicolations on the top of a donjon keep. A social *impasse* checked us at the foot. We all wanted to climb up to Acoma; we all had suit-cases. Might innocent pale-face suit-cases in an open Dodge car dwell for a few hours safely alone among prowling Red Indians?

"Bury 'em," suggested Beebo, and this we began to do. But, glancing up, we found every cliff knobby with the heads of surprised Indian onlookers observing this strange pale-face rite. So we left the suit-cases looking rather silly, up to their middles in sand, the cynosure of all Acoma eyes.

The sand-dune, leaning at a steep angle against the *mesa*, made heavy climbing. We sank calf-deep at every step and were glad when we came to the niches cut in the cliff, each foot-niche supplemented by neat hand-niches, which made climbing comparatively easy.

At the top of the cliff Frank awaited us, in his capacity of Acting Governor of Acoma. Frank had the rather horse-like flat-eyed look characteristic of his race. His heavy black hair was not shingled—it swept his shoulders. On his head he wore a broad sombrero and, on the rest of him, blue dungarees. His wife was very stout and wore a light chemise and the two long plaits of her hair. The other ladies of his family, in coloured blankets, were bent forward under the weight of babies strapped to their backs—bent forward so that their black plaits swung free before their breasts.

Frank led us most courteously round the village of Acoma. The houses had three storeys, arranged in three steps as children might pile wooden bricks—a short brick on a long brick and a little cube brick on the top of that. Each storey housed a family. To reach Frank's house we climbed a ladder to the first floor and found ourselves in a little front yard; here we were faced by another little house and flanked by ovens like beehives. By another ladder we climbed to the roof of that house and found an even smaller front yard and an even smaller house—Frank's house. Frank's wife was painting black squirls and squiggles on roughly-shaped baked white pots. The little cubic house was beautifully clean; the beds were niches in the mud wall with Navajo blankets in them; there were windows with splintery foggy mica panes. On the walls hung the family jewellery, chains of roughly wrought silver and turquoise. Hanging on the wall, too, were Frank's robe of office—a dainty thing of cherry-red tulle—and a walking-stick that had belonged to Abraham Lincoln. Lincoln had seven walking-sticks and he gave one to each of the self-governing Indian pueblos.

Frank took us to see the church, which dates back to Spanish times. The Spaniards, when they first crossed the desert, left a priest behind with orders to save Acoma's soul. Beebo told us that the people of Acoma did not at first appreciate the necessity of having their souls saved. Indeed, they pushed the priest over the edge of the cliff. He was, however, carrying an umbrella at the time, having imported cautious European habits into a country where it only rains about once in forty years. The umbrella unfurled and the priest, clinging to the crook and no doubt congratulating himself on his forethought, floated so slowly to desert level that the astounded citizens of Acoma were there to meet him when he landed. There they were, lying on their noses in honour of the miracle. The priest might have formed a limited company for the patenting and exploitation of the parachute—instead, he built a church. It is as if Sir Isaac Newton had merely eaten the apple and praised God for it instead of discovering gravitation. At any rate there is the church in Acoma still, a yellow mud church with towers like ears. And it is evident that the repentant converts gave of their best effort good measure, for only Indians could have designed and executed those mud gargoyles. The results of the priest's flight, therefore, endure to this day, for, ever since, a priest has visited Acoma regularly to conduct mass—and, ever since, no doubt, the police of Acoma have removed umbrellas from their criminals before pushing them over. "For if folks don't act right," said Beebo, "they push 'em over, same as then."

"All Acoma folks very good," insisted Frank with a deprecatory smile, as he exchanged glances with a demoniac gargoyle.

GEOGRAPHY

North Africa, close up on the starboard side, was made of shadows, and there were little towns drowning in the shadows. The tide on the lonely ochre cliffs went up and down with nobody to mark its changes, it seemed. In the coves there were little white beaches where no baby had ever set spade. Any unknown, little-visited land across a few miles of sea is very exciting; every shore, seen so, means to me a fine but impossible hope registered in that part of the brain that makes fine but hopeless plans. "If ever I have a home it will be among pale inhuman beaches like those; if ever I have babies, they shall slide on tea-trays down sand-dunes that have only been trailed before by reverent warm winds; we'll find strange berries among the grey shrubs that veil those mountain sides; we'll watch extraordinary little animals on the pockety yellow alps near those summits, and we'll go home in the evening through an uneven pale-pink village to a heavy tea in a wide Moorish house with thick, cool, plastered walls...."

The glamorous band of sea is a barrier across which thoughts of climate, mosquitoes, servant troubles and sanitation cannot come to me.

There is a crying need for imagination-geography in our schools. The text-books of that lovely science would be silent on the subject of exports and imports, principal bays and capes, watersheds and the mileage of rivers; such details as flora and fauna would have other and more adventurous headings and names. All the *feelings* of lands and seas would rise like a scent from between the pages.

As it is, few people know or love geography. Soldiers and sailors, of course, walk about the world on chunks of geography; they become expert in spite of themselves, and often their knowledge exhales that essence of the *feeling* of the far paths they have followed—that glory of very-far-away that I call imagination-geography. But of the women and civilians on board our P. & O., a good many were not aware what continent lay sunnily south of us—(poor Africa, one would have thought that by now it had done enough to make its mark!)—hardly anybody but the captain knew when we were looking at Portugal and when at Spain; we passed Cape St. Vincent without being able to find out what happened there and why and if so who won; we mistook Gibraltar for an island, and no doubt some of us insulted it by calling it Crete or the Crimea or St. Michael's Mount.

At least we all know something about Malta now. The very babies now on board will wake up and correct the teacher when Malta is mentioned during future geography lessons. They will not remember the exports and imports, but they will see again the hooded women and the goats.

Valetta, from the sea, is like a beehive. Except for a few steeples, turrets and cupolas, there is nothing to interrupt the close-built curve of the steep hill-encrusting city. Horizontal lines, built into pyramids, dominate the whole island of Malta; all the houses are as flat and square-cornered as bricks. There is scarcely any colour but cream-gold in all Valetta.

It was a national holiday when we arrived. The Maltese have a long memory; they still, it seems, make merry over the semi-miraculous raising of a siege in the sixteenth century. In the yellow shadows of the diving narrow streets the townspeople were rejoicing; banners were strung across the narrow chasms of the streets. Each gay perspective was stoppered at the far end by blue sea. The church bells rejoiced; they rang as urgently as firebells. Only in the great church of the Knights of Malta it was quiet. There, there was so much colour that one hardly missed the sunlight. But outside one was dazzled again. The women, hooded and mantled in black, sat on the church steps, and they alone were serenely shaded from the sun. Their great hoods were stiffened so as to lie—a horizontal yard of starched black—on their heads. There was room for a baby or two in the generous shade. The cloaks of the women hung curtained from this broad winged hood. Faces look beautiful so shadowed.

The milkman of Malta is the goatherd; the goats carry their milk themselves. The goats rustle down the rocky pathways and along the narrow steep streets and across the wide places on which grindstones stand like prehistoric petrified mushrooms. When a customer appears the goats stand patiently browsing on dust while the goatherd milks into the customer's own vessel—which is generally a demobilised beer or whisky-bottle.

We mounted a frail-looking cab drawn by a sad horse with a very long plume standing between its ears. We drove to the Hal-saflieni Hypogeum simply because we wanted to know what it was. We found catacombs said to be nearly five thousand years old. Behind a man with a lantern we filed down a winding stone stairway and through a long tangled series of dreadful caves. There were red paintings on the very low domed ceilings—or perhaps they were only stains of blood from the lacerated skulls of tourists who forgot to stoop. Dark cavities, like murderers' snares for doomed innocence, were set between square-hewn pillars. There was a wide well in which the water was still sweet. There was an altar ready, even now, for sacrifice. There were the skull, arms and ribs of a five-thousand-year-ago man, buried in an upright position. Seven thousand skeletons have been found in the catacombs.

After about twenty minutes in the fierce gaping maw of Malta, one was convinced that one would never see daylight again. And then, into one of the sepulchral shafts, daylight struck and, looking upward, one saw the shell of the prim innocent Victorian villa which, for generations, has stood all unaware above this dark secret. Generations of respectable persons admired those wallpapers, leaned from those window-frames, passed tamely across those gaping thresholds, while all the time beneath their feet the pagan old altar waited hungry for sacrifice, waited among the bones of seven thousand men.

ANGELS IN THE RED SEA

The Red Sea was red-hot. What wind there was, moved at the same speed as we did and counted for nothing. We wandered about pursuing ghosts of rumours of breezes as sceptically and as conscientiously as members of the Society for Psychical Research. The ghosts had always been laid by the time we arrived and, in honour of their memory, we sat and hated one another. A cube of hot sticky Red Sea was confined in a canvas tank on the lower deck; the tank was designed to hold three thin passengers or two and a half fat ones, but we crushed irritably into it six at a time.

We hated one another, yet we could not escape from our fellows.

I imagined a crowd of harassed guardian angels in the bows. Every passenger—even every unblessed steerage passenger—was represented in that company. The angels of the officers, the stewards, and the Lascars, if they existed, had their quarters elsewhere. The angels of the children were never seated for more than twenty seconds before, with a murmured, "Excuse me," they hurried away to meet some urgent need. The angels of the few good were sleepy and complacent. Old Mrs. Purey's guardian, indeed, was never in demand at all, except when his charge dropped a stitch or mislaid her spectacles. He was immensely stout, and affected the philosophical, innocuously epigrammatic manner common to those on whom the world makes no claim.

"It must be the heat," said Young Taylor's angel, who had shocked innocent eyes. "I can't keep my man up to his standards at all. He's holding Mrs. Wellington's hand now and I can't find a trace of Mabel on his conscience. Yet when they parted at Tilbury...." He hurried away again towards the promenade deck.

"It'll be hotter yet," giggled pretty Mrs. Wellington's angel. "But Mrs. W. and I have been this way seven times and we're acclimatised.

Young Taylor hasn't made any impression on us, I need hardly say. Nobody has since—well, we must amuse ourselves somehow...."

"Quite right," agreed Mrs. Purey's fat angel. "Happiness is a duty. Some people put happiness on and off like a robe. It should be rooted within, like bones."

Bennet's angel laughed abruptly. He had a white sour face and, like Bennet himself, carried a little flask. "Happiness ..." he said. "A duty? We worked that out twenty years ago." He sipped from his flask. "Yes, happiness, as you say, should be rooted warmly among the tired bones...."

Tetherton's angel was obviously accustomed to elementary military life. "Oh *that* method doesn't pay," he said, and he had caught from his subaltern, Tetherton, the throaty guilty manner of one trying to uphold high principles of which he is ashamed. "It's a man's duty and all that, if you know what I mean, to keep decent and fit and what not ...especially before natives."

The heat wove trembling coils of air between the ship and the burnt, corrugated coast. The still air touched one's lips like fever.

Young Taylor's angel reappeared irritably in front of Tetherton's. "Hasn't your man got anything better to do than annoy mine? It isn't funny, though it seems to make Mrs. Wellington laugh. We can't help it if our Adam's apple *is* a little prominent." His temper flared suddenly. "Don't you see that he hates himself enough already? You make him feel *all* Adam's apple in Mrs. Wellington's sight. Oh yes, he's forgotten Mabel now—and your man can only make silly jokes...."

"Oh well, my man's only ragging. Can't you stand a little fun? It's hot and we must work our energy off. Come along with me and settle things."

Mrs. Wellington's angel giggled again. "But Taylor is simply a *sketch*, isn't he? Anyway it's too hot to be kind."

"It'll be hotter yet," said Mrs. Purey's angel placidly. "How glad I am that my old woman knits so much. She is rising to heaven on a life-line of heather-mixture wool. But if I were you, dear, I'd run along and give your Mrs. Wellington a hint."

"Pff ... as if she couldn't look after herself!"

The ship rolled a little in the slow blue sea. A rim of white ran up and down the parched, unvisited beaches of Arabia. A couple of whales in the distance flung up light fans of spray. A great noise of hot babies, crying drearily, haunted the air. Behind that noise there was, it seemed, a soundless roar of heat to deafen hearts. A sensation of dreadful excitement was poised on the deck.

Tetherton's angel came back, limp with sullenness. "It really *is* your job," he said to Mrs. Wellington's angel. "I can't control my man while your woman eggs him on."

Taylor's angel followed him furiously. "Call your man off. Call him off, or there'll be murder. Stop him grinning with his gums like that. We're cleverer than he is, though we never went to public school. Mabel loves us.... Call your man off."

"Oh, stow it—it's only fun," shouted Tetherton's angel, whose face was scarlet. "Does the silly ass imagine that Mrs. Wellington ever had any use for him anyway?"

The heat jerked their features and limbs absurdly. They jostled each other like furious children as they ran back to their charges. Mrs. Purey's angel suddenly looked alarmed. "Why ... why ... she's stopped knitting...." He waddled away. Soon all were gone except Bennet's angel and Mrs. Wellington's.

"I simply must go and watch the row," said Mrs. Wellington's angel, after fidgeting for a little while. "I'm not going to interfere, of course. *I'm* not to blame if they choose to make fools of themselves. I believe they'll murder each other before night."

Before night! There was a great brass wall of day to climb before night.

Bennet did not need his angel. He had found a kind of peace. He was asleep by the door of the bar. A sunbeam, refracted through an empty glass, explored his crumpled figure as the ship rolled. For a long time Bennet's angel sat watching the sea. Like fairies over a troubled city, the flying-fish sprang from the eaves of the waves and flew with a lilt till they slipped down distant white chimneys of spray. In pursuit of the ship came the dolphins, so near that one could see the trembling steel strength of their bodies, as they curved themselves— taut as bows—in the air.

Perim was in sight. A gag upon the mouth of the dead Red Sea. A scarred island crushed with heat. A terrible sleek island enclosed in a brazen crust of heat, as a more fortunate island might be enclosed in a shell of trees and flowers. The round oil-tanks watched the sky with an insane stare.

Mrs. Wellington's angel came back. "Oh, my dear, Taylor and Tetherton had a fight. I *knew* they would. Taylor said, 'I'll kill you for that,' and Tetherton danced about squawking, 'Kamerad,' and with his toe unhitched Taylor's deck-chair so that Taylor sat with a bang among the ruins.... Oh, my *dear*, I thought we'd have *died* ... he looked so comic. And they fought and their angels fought and—what do you think?—Mrs. Purey let her knitting drop and upped and boxed Taylor's ears—you should have seen her old angel's face as he pulled her off. The knitting fell into the sea. Three of the flappers are in hysterics and the captain says he'll put Taylor in irons. And my Mrs. W.'s gone down to her cabin all of a dither. She'll be joyful and excited over her old letters for the next hour or so—pretending it isn't true that the man who wrote them died at Ypres.... What's your man doing?"

"Still asleep. Still asleep."

The island of Perim passed slowly, and, behind it, the charred mountains of the mainland revolved, moving in and out of clouds. The polished sea between the ship and Perim was scratched by the fins of sharks and pocked by shoals of leaping fish.

And suddenly the wind and the world came into that hot void. A terrible doubt seemed dispelled by the gay wind. The cords of presentiment and doom slipped from the strangled throat of the day. The air was clean of cries and of the drumming of heat. A cool crown of serenity clasped the foreheads of the angels as they returned in quiet groups.

"The hand of the heat has let us go," said Bennet's angel, rising a little unsteadily to meet them. "We were prisoners. We are free. Good-bye."

"Why—where are you going?"

"I'm taking my man home."

"Home? But isn't he due to land to-morrow at Aden?"

"Land? What is land to him now? I'm taking him home."

PICNIC IN ADEN

Aden was on fire—at least, every sense but the eye told one so. If one shut one's eyes, flames seemed to crackle against one's quivering skin, but in sight there were only yellow forked mountains like flames trembling against the brassy sky. In several Ford cars we drove through Aden and the hot breath of the fiery mountains roared about us.

We were undergoing a picnic, in search of a breeze. It was our duty to go first to the tanks and then to the oasis. Residents in Aden consider their tanks very interesting. Probably all the inhabitants of Aden go up on Fords or camels to look at their tanks every day, and congratulate one another on having stuff like that to look at in a place where it never rains. Every time they have a bath they swell with pride, I expect. And now and then, on very great occasions, they drink a little water as a great treat. The camels, I am sure, do not sympathise with the demonstrations of enthusiasm at the tanks' edge. Camels, it is said, drink only about three drops of water a month. They have the faces of typical prohibitionists. They look like traditional school-marms; they carry their heads at an angle that suggests sour prudishness; they compress their long hare-lips; their bulging eyes are forever shocked and frigid. All goods and vehicles in Aden, except the ubiquitous Ford cars, are carried or drawn by camels. Probably Fords have to appeal to them too sometimes, when they break down on the steep hills. Camels would enjoy those occasions. They would enjoy saying, "I told you so." You can see they are always shocked because the Fords wear no fur.

The desert around Aden imitates water; on all sides imaginary water shimmers. Water seems to have flooded the pathetic golf-links of baked, bladeless desert; far-off native villages seem to stand in lakes among their silvery reflections. There is no water really, and its semblance only intensifies the glare. The hot wind dries up the mockery of coolness.

Our faithful boiling Fords are assembling at their destination. Here, in the oasis, fainting trees are planted in the sand. There is a summer-house. There is even an embryonic Zoo—for this is a pleasure resort. We drape ourselves limply about the cages of three gazelles— (of the kind "I never loved")—four dog-faced baboons and a porcupine. A heroic steward has kept a piece of ice alive all the way from the ship; it dies now ineffectually in tepid ginger beer. Why have we come? The porcupine looks at us in surprise and shrugs its shoulders with a cynical rattle of quills. There is distant thunder. In Aden, I believe, you can distinguish the rainy season from the dry season by the fact that, during the former, distant thunder can be heard twice a week.

The weaver-birds' nests hang by long strong threads from the branches. The nests are quite round and exquisitely woven; their doors, pierced at a downward angle, escape the sun and catch the air. Weaver-birds, in natural pride, strut about giving little lectures on their art. But we are too hot to be instructed.

Shall we go back to the ship? At least it couldn't be hotter. We remember the ship sentimentally; there was once a corner, aft of the deck-tennis net, where someone once felt a little breath of air. We reach the quay; the ship looks like heaven, so tall and pale-summited upon the lapping cool water, her decks capped by awnings, the shadow of her hull churned by diving-boys and boats full of ostrich feathers.

"Have-a-dive.... Dive-for-shilling.... Look, lady, very fine feather only fifteen rupee...." It is a hot clamour, overloading the fainting air. Perhaps our oasis was cooler after all. Surely the weaver-birds' nests were swinging a little.... Have we fled from the only breeze in the world?

YUNNAN—I

Yunnan is a forgotten province, a piece of China mislaid by the world. Yunnan has declared itself independent, but I do not suppose the world heard the declaration very clearly. You cannot get to Yunnanfu, the capital of Yunnan, from the China side, without riding for a month or so on a donkey, and somehow revolutions and declarations are not very impressive when made by places to which the approach is so humble and so tedious.

But there is a quicker way to Yunnanfu—you have to leave China to find it. From Hongkong you take a pig-boat to Haiphong, in Tonkin; from Haiphong a little harum-scarum French train carries you up for three days towards the sky. You must spend two steamy and flea-bitten nights in little primitive inns. The first day you wriggle like a worm through close wet jungles of bananas and bamboos and oozy palms and snaky creepers. The second day your train cleaves red-wealed mountains. And on the third day you follow a red river along plumed ravines. The river is a little disciple of the Yang-tse. On its face I could see, in little, all the tricks and fantasies the Yang-tse had first shown me—the glaze of intense swiftness on vivid water, the cream-filled bowls of the whirlpools, the frozen wave that hangs over a rock in mid-rapids, the different levels and contrary impulses of tortured water. The river has done the work of a genie for the French engineers who built the railway; it has moved mountains, it has carved deep gorges, it has bound beetling rocks together with the roots of trees on slopes so steep that a bird in the crest of one tree can sing to a mouse burrowing in the roots of another. The train fears rocks no more than it stops for a bird's singing; it simply takes advantage of the work of the fairy river, occupying itself irresponsibly in leaping from side to side of rapids by means of thin hopeful bridges.

Yunnanfu has a big forty-mile-long lake the colour of a dark pearl. Along the high sides of the mountains that border this lake goes the train, freed at last of its dependence on the river, through orchards and at last across a broad well-cultivated tableland pricked with poplars— to arrive at Yunnanfu, a common, crowded railway station under a low dull sky that hides the mountains.

Yunnanfu is an independent city, even its climate—at 6000 feet up—scorns compromise. The city must be sought, it will not welcome you. Outside the walls one may find all the things that never need to be sought—a club, a French-Greek hotel, cocktails, hospitable men who make jocosities about "the ladies". But at the gate of Yunnanfu one enters a China that is difficult and rare, and one does not easily leave it again, for it is a great city. It must be very great, for it contains half a continent.

In the city everyone in the streets should be looked at as intently as oneself is looked at by everyone. For in Yunnanfu every citizen is charming to the eyes. The tribeswomen are gaunt and handsome; their dress is as gay as lanterns in the narrow shady streets. The typical woman wears a faded mauve or rose-red tunic, bright blue or green trousers, white ankle-puttees, and pointed curved embroidered shoes, mounted on thick short extra soles like pattens. She is Lo-lo, not Chinese, so her feet are not bound. On her head she wears a blue square of cotton as a hood and, balanced askew on the top of the hood, a tiny-crowned, big-brimmed straw hat which is kept in position by a silver chain buckled under the chin. Her baby sprawls, crab-like, against her back in a big gaudy handkerchief; its little hands and feet, with silver bangles on wrists and ankles, dangle at the four corners of the handkerchief; its placid sleepy dirty face, against the nape of its mother's neck, is framed in a fierce-eyed, whiskered tiger hat.

The tribespeople of Yunnan, of whom the Lo-los form the majority, are despised by the Chinese. The Chinese call them dogs and profess to believe that, when they wear kilts, it is to conceal their tails. But, remembering cities of Yunnan, one seems always to have seen Chinese sitting on chairs looking at nothing, Chinese lying on beds smoking opium, Chinese looking on at quarrels, Chinese riding nervously on led ponies—and Lo-los always working. The short sturdy women of the tribes—swinging their kilts as they stride in groups on bare strong shapely legs, their rosy weather-beaten faces framed by the great loads they carry—do not deserve the patronising sneer of the Chinese city woman, trussed in gaudy figured satin, tottering on helpless crushed feet under her crimson and yellow deep-frilled umbrella of false modesty.

On the air of Yunnanfu rings nearly always the clanking of prisoners' chains. Everywhere there are prisoners, ankle chained to ankle, repairing the cobbled alley-ways, carrying loads of earth or cans of water, cursing and prodding the slow oxen and buffaloes which draw waggons whose wheels are never round. Nearly all the real work of the city runs to the wretched tune of chains. The men are mostly brigands serving the ends of a rare justice. If all the brigands in that district were at large there would be no room to move upon the mountains, so the authorities have to step in now and then to relieve over-crowding of the foremost local industry.

Once in the early morning I was awakened by the marching clank of little treble chains—and there were the baby brigands shuffling by, of any age from seven to fifteen, thin and in rags, ankle dragging sore chained ankle, but all chattering shrilly.

A funeral is a far gayer thing to meet. There was one at which the dead man's pony assisted, all done up in white paper frills like a ham. The male mourners were swathed in white and wore on their heads superstructures like rows of white croquet-hoops springing from brow to nape. Though apparently quite cheerful and well, each was laboriously supported by a coolie and by a staff rosetted with paper flowers. The widow, though in orthodox white, must walk unsupported, like the pony. Behind her came a crowd of gay chattering women in their brightest and best satin brocades, tight trousers and embroidered peg-top shoes.

But even if there were no citizens in Yunnanfu, there would always be the chance at every corner of meeting very strange strangers—at this junction of caravan routes from Burma, from Tibet, from Western China or the North.

Outside a booth I met a travelling priest. He was very tall and wore a flippant Dolly Varden type of hat, tilted forward, bent down in front and up behind—or rather the brim of the hat was Dolly Varden, the crown was absent. The space where the crown should have been was occupied by the priest's own shaven skull rising neatly through the hole and encircled by a blue band, a rudimentary turban. The man wore an immense quilted coat, not in the least ragged, but exquisitely patched all over in white and various shades of blue. Even his shoes were made of little blue and white shreds neatly pieced together. He carried a tall staff and a begging bowl. In contrast with that huge jig-

113

saw man, the crazy street—a-dazzle with gold signs and swinging lanterns, lintels painted with birds, eaves alive with dolphins, dark
gatehouses guarded by elephants and watching with one hot red cyclo-
pean painted eye—all looked suddenly sane.

In Mengtsz, Yunnan, half-way between Yunnanfu and Tonkin, we
came to live. In Mengtsz I found myself settling down domestically
for the first time in my life, going to market as though I were a housewife in Putney, S.W.

On ponies and on foot, in buffalo-carts and ox-carts, with or without captive pigs, ducks, chickens, foxes, or leopards, every one is
coming into Mengtsz market through the dark gate that pierces the
thick wall of the city. Tribespeople have come for miles from the re-
moter mountains, some loaded, some carrying nothing more than a
couple of onions and a persimmon for sale. The tribespeople have
wrinkled, humorous faces; some of them have fair hair and grey eyes;
the features of most look more Western than Eastern. Some of them
look like little Greek soldiers in their lilting kilts. Some wear wide
leather bands, thickly studded with silver, round their heads, some
have broad blue embroidered sun-bonnets and aprons caught with silver buckles at the shoulders, some have their own thick hair bound
with silver coils and silk into a big turban, from which a cascade of
hair escapes over each ear. Some wear enormous dark-blue turbans,
tight jackets with sailor collars and striped sleeves, and—hitching up
the hem of the jackets behind—curious prominent mid-Victorian bus-
tles. Some wear black and scarlet strappings picked out in silver on
short sleeveless tunics, and these look much more military than the
soldiers, who slouch about in dirty grey cotton uniforms on thin,
bandy, stockinged legs.

The Annamites move in the crowd, immigrants from Tonkin on
the heels of the French. They always wear chestnut brown or black
with a touch of scarlet or apple-green, and their black turbans are very
neat and close under their huge balanced straw hats. A respectable
Annamite woman keeps her teeth enamelled black, and the smile on
her rather pretty pale face is thereby made atrocious, like a gash.

There is hardly room to move in the market. Only the buffaloes,
by sheer weight, can make room. The buffaloes crawl in long obstruc-
tive strings through the cramped streets; they look at nothing, they turn
aside for nothing. Housewife from London, S.W., and Lo-lo chief
alike may find themselves trundled ignominiously along from behind
by those broad blunt horns. The buffalo's head is wedged into his

114

yoke, so perhaps he cannot take an intelligent interest in the world, and perhaps the cart that he draws, with its two massive sections of un-trimmed log for wheels, is rather like a Juggernaut car, and bumps his poor tail if he pauses to consider the claims of other marketers.

The dogs are all out marketing; they lay in stores and never pay their bills, except in the bruises and sores that result from kicks and blows. Nothing that cannot speak is gently treated in Mengtsz. The chickens, alive, are hung up by their feet, and groan hoarsely in unchicken-like voices; the carp gasp desperately in parched masses; the limbs of the ponies and donkeys bleed and tremble beneath great burdens, and some ponies walk on deformed ankles, the hoofs being turned up in front like skis. But children, though very much in the way on such a busy day, are always loved; little babies are strapped on the backs of their tired shrill mothers, and older babies are carried on proud fathers' arms. There is a ragged beggar carrying on his back his very aged mother—a knotted grey dreadful figure in an aura of flutter-ing rags and grey hair; her brown bare skeleton legs point stiffly forward from beneath her good son's arms. There is a blind beggar who crashes his bleeding head against the cobble-stones as he shrieks for alms, another who twines the bony footless stump of his leg round his neck in order to earn a copper from us.

Also from Benediction Books ...
Wandering Between Two Worlds: Essays on Faith and Art
Anita Mathias
Benediction Books, 2007
152 pages
ISBN: 0955373700

Available from www.amazon.com, www.amazon.co.uk

In these wide-ranging lyrical essays, Anita Mathias writes, in lush, lovely prose, of her naughty Catholic childhood in Jamshedpur, India; her large, eccentric family in Mangalore, a sea-coast town converted by the Portuguese in the sixteenth century; her rebellion and atheism as a teenager in her Himalayan boarding school, run by German missionary nuns, St. Mary's Convent, Nainital; and her abrupt religious conversion after which she entered Mother Teresa's convent in Calcutta as a novice. Later rich, elegant essays explore the dualities of her life as a writer, mother, and Christian in the United States-- Domesticity and Art, Writing and Prayer, and the experience of being "an alien and stranger" as an immigrant in America, sensing the need for roots.

About the Author

Anita Mathias is the author of *Wandering Between Two Worlds: Essays on Faith and Art.* She has a B.A. and M.A. in English from Somerville College, Oxford University, and an M.A. in Creative Writing from the Ohio State University, USA. Anita won a National Endowment of the Arts fellowship in Creative Nonfiction in 1997. She lives in Oxford, England with her husband, Roy, and her daughters, Zoe and Irene.

Visit Anita's website
http://www.anitamathias.com,
and Anita's blog
http://dreamingbeneaththespires.blogspot.com, (Dreaming Beneath the Spires).

The Church That Had Too Much
Anita Mathias
Benediction Books, 2010
52 pages
ISBN: 9781849026567

Available from www.amazon.com, www.amazon.co.uk

The Church That Had Too Much was very well-intentioned. She wanted to love God, she wanted to love people, but she was both hampered by her muchness and the abundance of her possessions, and beset by ambition, power struggles and snobbery. Read about the surprising way The Church That Had Too Much began to resolve her problems in this deceptively simple and enchanting fable.

About the Author

Anita Mathias is the author of *Wandering Between Two Worlds: Essays on Faith and Art.* She has a B.A. and M.A. in English from Somerville College, Oxford University, and an M.A. in Creative Writing from the Ohio State University, USA. Anita won a National Endowment of the Arts fellowship in Creative Nonfiction in 1997. She lives in Oxford, England with her husband, Roy, and her daughters, Zoe and Irene.

Visit Anita's website
  http://www.anitamathias.com,
and Anita's blog
  http://dreamingbeneaththespires.blogspot.com (Dreaming Beneath the Spires).

www.ingramcontent.com/pod-product-compliance
Lightning Source LLC
Chambersburg PA
CBHW030519100426
42813CB00001B/92